All the Things

Kristen L. Schindler

Cara ~
Thank you for your book
support! May this book
encourage you to know
we are all in this mothering
journey together!
♡ Kristen Schindler

DEDICATION

I dedicate this book to my husband and children who have
made the fabric of my life stronger, richer, warmer, funnier, and
more beautiful. Thank you to all my friends and extended family
for your sweet words of encouragement on this journey. Thank
you for walking by my side even when I couldn't always clearly
see God's plan.

Most importantly, I dedicate this book to my sweet
momma, Karen, who has dedicated her entire life to her family.
She has taught me everything I know about being steadfast, true,
and faithful to those she loves. Thank you for your unwavering
support and always loving me "to the moon and back."

CONTENTS

ACKNOWLEDGMENTS

I want to thank my husband, Eric, for always encouraging me to share my heart. For twenty years you told me to put myself out there. You have continued to gently support me and this vision even when it seemed a little blurry from my perspective.

To my dad, Jerry, thank you for being my chief editor. Your voracious love for all things books and grammar related is a true gift. I am blessed to have your mastery of both mind and pen on this journey. It has been a gift to work with you on this book.

Special thanks to my bestie, Elisa, who has been a constant spiritual strength and support during our years of shared motherhood. You are an eternal blessing to me and my heart.

To my dear chosen sister, Jenny, thank you for always being my safe listening ear and taking me to glorious mountain lakes where I could breathe deeply and find myself again.

To my sister, Tiffany, thank you for always being an encourager, reminding me of what's important, and letting me be my authentic self.

To my Gram, thank you for always being supportive, praying for me, and always loving me.

To all the other mommas, friends, and family who have filled my spirit and soul, your words of support are priceless. You have encouraged me to be brave. You have helped breathe life into this project so it could take flight so other mommas can feel the safety net and supportive web of connection.

To my dear children, Gavin, Logan, and Ava, thank you for being patient when I was diving so deeply and immersed in the birth of this project. Being your mom has been the biggest joy of my life. Your hearts remind me of what it is all about. Know that you were each created with a divine purpose and equally unique gifts to take you where you need to go. Keep your eyes open for those paths to emerge and when you see them, bravely step forward knowing God is covering you and I am cheering you on. Never stop believing in and being the good in the world. You are loved beyond measure, and I love you more.

1
ALL THE THINGS

Sixteen years ago, with a swollen belly and cravings for seedless watermelon and lemonade, I entered a new world. This world was one that I naively thought I had prepared myself for.

I consulted professionals and had numerous conversations with other women who had gone before me. Some of them gave such great advice and encouragement. Their words gave my "soon to be a momma's" heart such peace. I could spend hours with these mommas listening to their ways of handling things and the outlooks they had about all that motherhood encompassed. They were a perfect combination of "mother earth" and the best Pinterest has to offer.

All the Things

Then there were *the others*. Their stories were raw, and their feelings were so amplified that I wanted to leave their company as fast as I saw them. Their energy was high, but their stories were ones that didn't give me peace. They gave me anxiety. They talked about how tired they were. They spoke of something called "peeing in peace" and they wished they could have it.

Was this really a problem? Honestly! Surely, these mommas were the dramatic ones in high school who always coated their stories with a little added embellishment for good measure. So, I pushed those stories away and figured that those mommas were just merely the "exception." Oh, what a naive momma I was.

You see, I thought that I was prepared for this journey. I compared the journey I was going to undertake to someone heading out for a major camping and hiking trip. I mean, Babies R Us is like a glorified outdoor camping trip store, right? They both have beds, bathing contraptions, food storage, dried snacks, and clothing for various needs. I mean women have been bearing children since the beginning. How different could this adventure with a tiny human being actually be?

Preparation is the key to any big trip or adventure. Why would this one be any different? I had read all the books. I knew what to physically expect. All the ointments, creams, pads, and undergarments were organized in bins. I watched all the shows and the birth plan was all set. I mapped it all out like a highlighted Rand McNally Road Atlas that was prepped for an epic trip.

In addition, I had all the things that a baby would need. The clothes were washed and folded neatly. The glider was covered in a matching fabric to the crib. The books I would tenderly read my new lovebug were neatly stacked, their spines were arranged biggest to smallest. The diapers in various sizes were stacked and ready for the many changes each day. The bouncy seats, baby swings, and gates were all at the ready.

In my mind, I had ALL THE THINGS.

All the Things

Oh, but sweet sister, what I didn't know then that I do know now is ALL THE THINGS you need aren't really "things" you can touch at all.

After sixteen years of being on this journey, I have found ALL THE THINGS are so much more than the books, diapers, backpacks, strollers, sippy cups, shoes, and supplies for camp. ALL THE THINGS are so much more than can be neatly packed in a backpack or nursery.

The real needs of a newly birthed momma are the things that fly and swirl in our tired momma heads. They are not able to be tied down and diapered.

ALL THE THINGS encompass every feeling you will feel, every longing you will have of your former self. The self that you left on the delivery table. You didn't want to leave her there, but it needed to be done. Some of us thought that we could hold on to her and that it was just the embellishments of "the others" that you lose yourself when you become a mother.

All the Things

But the truth is, just like its journey to become the butterfly, the caterpillar has to leave its once malleable soft body to become something that can fly. It retreats into its cocoon and probably reads all the "What to Expect When Turning from a Caterpillar to a Butterfly" books it can. It probably has watched all the episodes on the Insect Channel of those who have pupated before it.

But here's the thing. After the caterpillar emerges, it has to wait. It has to sit very still and take it all in. Its wings are so fragile that it needs to wait a while and let them dry. It needs to fully comprehend and right itself for this new adventure.

There is a sacred beauty in the transformation and birth of a mother. However, take the time to give yourself a minute. Right yourself on where you are now and the season in which you are flying. To keep up with this new life that was created, you will need to fly swiftly sister. You will need to swoop and glide.

You will also need to find the gentle breeze to float on when your wings are so tired they can't possibly carry you higher.

All the Things

And you will need to know where to go when you need the sweet nectar of encouragement and inspiration. When you find those flowers in your life, THESE ARE THE THINGS! Just sit still. Take them all in. Not to mention you will need to open and show the brilliant color of your unique wings. Other mommas will need to see there is beauty in differences although you all are searching for that sweet peace.

ALL THE THINGS are the friendships you crave despite the fact you haven't showered in two days. Or three days. Or you have lost count. They become the road map that will help you to navigate this journey. Some of those friends will have always been there and you will share a history of what you thought this journey was going to be like.

You will laugh at each other over coffee, wine, or Mountain Dew and wonder how you could have been so educated in many areas yet so ignorant in others.

Then there will be those who are new to your terrain. Some will feel so comfortable you are sure your souls have met before. They all have been pivotally placed to support, encourage, and pour into your momma journey.

ALL THE THINGS are the answers to the questions you have in the middle of the night and can't seem to find. They are the rabbit holes of worry that are so slippery you can't get a hold despite your best effort. They are all the fears that clog your mind when all you want is to fall asleep because the baby/toddler/teen is finally asleep, and you know tomorrow is only a few short hours away. Look to others who have traveled these paths and streams before you. Open your mouth and share that you feel lost and confused and the "key" on the map just doesn't seem to be making sense. That your compass is just not showing "true north" and you need a Sacagawea to help you navigate. They have the THINGS that will help you. They will help you navigate the current that seems too strong or help identify uncertain berries you aren't sure are safe.

ALL THE THINGS is the help you need with the invisible weights you carry that just never seem to get lighter or the "to do" lists that you are never able to check off completely. You will need to learn to put the weights down. You will need to learn that the "to do" lists are a constant, but their completion is not a definition of your success or failure as a mother. This isn't something we tend to do easily. We are like sponges that continue to just suck up more and more to do.

ALL THE THINGS are gentle voices of those who love you that will tell you to give yourself a break to regain your strength when life throws you into marathons you haven't trained or signed up for. Listen to those voices. Heed those voices even though you will balk at first and your feathers are all out of sorts. They are not condemning you or judging you even though this is your first reaction.

Rather they are like your own personal lifeguards who are seeing you struggle. They are on watch for your safety. You are keeping your head above water, but the flailing is not helping. The struggle is real and they see it while they sit on the sidelines. They have a different view. You can't see it from where you are.

All the Things

You are barely getting over each wave as it comes at you. They don't want you to go under, but when you do, they will throw you a buoy in the form of a home-cooked meal or a needed caffeine fix. Or maybe they will take your kids for you to get that shower in. After all, dry shampoo only works for so long sister.

My hope in writing this book is to share ALL THE THINGS I have learned so far that were never covered in all the books and shows. My time with my children is far from over and I surely have had some paths and trails that have been treacherous. I have lost my way, been discouraged, compared myself to others, lost my temper, and wished things were different.

I have wished that I could have one more day with the woman I was before this transformation started. I mean really. I had SO much free time I haphazardly squandered before this journey started. Surely, I should have invented something noteworthy or discovered the cure for something while peeing in peace. (The "others" weren't embellishers).

All the Things

With sharing these stories and pieces of my heart, I hope you will feel you are not alone. That you will see beauty, hope, and goodness surround us all if we are looking through the situation with the right perspective. That you might feel a sense of sisterhood in the intangible and ethereal needs we all share and then be able to give ALL THE THINGS to other mommas who are placed in your path. Because honestly, we all thought we would be good if we got our nurseries outfitted by showers and numerous trips to Target. Dear Sister, we were already so lost before even taking the first step.

2
THE CREATION OF A NON-JUDGMENTAL PARENT

Before I was a parent I judged. I judged a lot. I listened to how children whined in stores and vowed that mine would have a *good thing coming to them* if they dared to have that type of attitude. No ma'am! Not happening on my watch!

I saw boys with shorts on during cold weather and wanted to take them home with me. I wondered what type of parent they had not looking out for their child's skin on a chilly day. They were obviously being neglected! Where were protective services when you needed them? Probably the same place that cops are when cars are speeding by me on the interstate!

All the Things

I looked at the houses of friends with small children and wondered why they couldn't see the grimy dirt on bathroom walls. Hadn't they heard of Magic Erasers? Norwex? Come on people, get on board and get to work! I would drop by and see toys awry and bedrooms tangled with who knew what. Was that a banana peel under that night stand? I think I saw a string cheese wrapper too! People! Let's keep the clutter contained. What were these people thinking? It was like an episode of Hoarders: Parenthood edition.

Before I was a parent, I made promises I couldn't keep. My children would have home-cooked meals each night for dinner. We would sit down promptly when my husband got home and share a lovely dinner over conversation of what we all did that day. We would talk about the positive things that happened and perhaps the things we struggled with as well.

We would routinely bake cookies for no special reason and our Christmas cookies would ROCK! In addition, I would make sure to not be *that* parent who scrounges to get last minute supplies for school projects. There is no reason to procrastinate

after all. I was sure those lists of supplies went out in plenty of

time to be on top of my parenting game.

Our nighttime routine would follow the pediatric sleep

needs of children in the various ages they were. I vowed that my

kids would be in bed promptly by 8:00 p.m. on a school night.

They would be read to each night and feel snug in their beds

before they sweetly closed their eyes and went off to dreamland.

Before I was a parent, I had control issues. Blame it on my

birth order, circumstances of life, being a teacher, or plain DNA.

Whatever its root, I needed to be in control. From the beginning

of the journey of motherhood and being pregnant for the first

time, I wanted it all planned out.

I wanted to plan when I had the baby, time of year, time

taken off work, blah blah blah. It all seemed so smooth. This

would happen then, and life would be grand. The timetable was

color coded, the mapping highlighted, and everything was on

track.

Then I lost the baby.

That wasn't part of the plan.

That was a time for reevaluation. The first chapter of many in the new memoir of my life would become *Losing Control of the Life I Once Knew.* It was an illusion.

All of it.

Once I got pregnant again, my thoughts changed throughout my pregnancy. I knew it was a fragile time and I did not take it for granted because things could go wrong quickly. I took time to put my feet up, eat healthy, and take naps. I haven't had a nap without interruption since. That's sixteen and a half years and counting. Sleep deprivation is real sister!

Before my son made his appearance, I felt like, "Okay, I got this." All the baby gifts were organized, the clothes were put away, and the book shelf was stacked. We had an arsenal of wipes and diapers. I felt the ability to breathe. We were good. We were going to hit this parenting thing full force!

All the Things

Once my son arrived, I had a lot of help from my mom and my mother-in-law. My mom came and stayed for a couple of weeks and my mother-in-law would come to help as she lived about 45 minutes away.

Both had years of experience, and even though not all of what they were saying was mutually agreed upon, I appreciated their help. Our small intimate "village" was under construction. With their help, my husband and I would make it. We would survive this enigma called parenting a newborn.

Then the sleep deprivation kicked in.

*Note to those of you who are *not* parents yet. Sleep deprivation is no joke. It is par with Chinese water torture. Being tired is one thing. Being "Mommy-tired" is a completely different beast.

I now look back on those pre-mommy years and feel I truly should have done more for the greater good. What did I do with all that extra time? I surely could have started a charitable organization, donated more time for underprivileged youth, or found the cure for something.

I remember one day of sleep deprivation clearly, as it was the first official fight my husband and I had as new parents. Remembering anything clearly from that time is in fact quite an accomplishment in its own right.

Honestly, parenting a newborn is like navigating one long, three-month day. It is like you are waking from constant small naps. You never hit deep sleep and REM is really pushing it. The hours ebb and flow, one into the next, and you realize the last time you were up at 2:48 a.m. there were drinks and karaoke, and hot wings may or may not have been involved. I can't quite recall. Those pre-parenthood days are tricky memories. The vault is tightly sealed.

I believe it was day 30 of Camp Mommy-tired. My parents and grandparents were visiting to see our new little love bug. I was one-part ecstatic that my sweet little boy's grandparents and great grandparents were here to see him, and one part miserable

thinking my body might fall into 7 million pieces.

I was so tired that I couldn't even verbalize what I needed

when it was time to nurse the baby for the 45,734th time since the

day before yesterday.

I could clearly see what I needed. If I had magical mommy

powers, I could have projected the image from my brain to my

husband's. He would have been able to see the hologram clearly,

gone to the laundry, and retrieved the needed item. However, I

was new to this mommy gig.

There was nothing magical. The only unicorns and

rainbows I saw were because I was so sleep deprived. I don't

think they were really there.

I tried to use my words. They were few. He didn't get it.

Me: I need one of those things.

Him: One of those things???

Me: Yes. Those.

Him: What thing?

All the Things

Me: You know the thing that I use. (Insert big tired mom eyes here. They may or may not have been bulging out a bit like I had a thyroid issue starting.)

Him: You use for what?

Me: FOR THE BABY!

Him: Ok. No, I don't know. You use a lot of things! A diaper?

Me: No.

Him: A wipe?

Me: (indignantly) NO! You know the thing that I put on my shoulder, the thing that I use!

Him: Why don't you just tell me what it is that you need? I'm not a mindreader!

Me: I AM TELLING YOU!!! I NEED THE THING THAT I USE FOR THE BABY!!!!

It was at this time that my bulging bug eyes brimmed with tears. I tried to say *all the words*. It didn't matter. I had nothing more.

All the Things

Needless to say, he found the thing.

It was a burp cloth. That was the exact thing I had been trying to get across to him. Why he couldn't catch the clue bird sooner I have no idea. Could it possibly be that he too was a comatose sleepwalker in a daddy suit?

At this point, grace was not something I was giving freely to anyone.

It was in the laundry.

The burp cloth was there with all the other burp cloths that had been so neatly folded, organized, and stacked only four weeks prior. Our projectile burping baby made quick use of those bad boys.

The lesson here is I was so sleep deprived I couldn't even pull that vocabulary word from my brain. I could see the burp cloth. I could feel the burp cloth. But to put that word into sounds that made sense. *Nope*. Me, a seasoned lover of words, Scrabble player, and impromptu poet and rhymer found it hard to function. My brain was GONE.

All the Things

So why do I tell you this story? Well for one, it was the first time I felt the control slipping as a new parent. I mean, I couldn't even speak coherently. Now, sixteen years into this extravaganza we call parenting, I have changed a lot and many other things have slipped along the way.

First of all, my children have all had attitudes and been sassy in stores. They have hidden in the clothes racks as I frantically called their names through gritted teeth. They have fought over who gets to push the cart, or sit in the cart, or hold the side of the cart. Sweet Jesus, it's not a ride at Six Flags!

I have felt the eyes of judgment at Target and Walmart. I remember clearly when my four-year-old had a meltdown at the checkout because I wouldn't give her candy. I smiled at the cashier and other people in line and said, "It's hard being 4. I mean heck, it's hard being 40!" And now, instead of judging those other mothers, I look at them, smile, and say, "Keep going, Momma! Hang in there!" I also try to distract their crazed babe so my fellow momma can load her groceries and get the heck out of there.

Secondly, my children don't always wear appropriate clothing when we leave the house. If it is hot outside, they dress like it's the arctic. If it is sleeting, they act like they are catching a trip to the Caribbean. Just today, we headed to meet a group of friends to go swim at the local Y. We were under a heat advisory for the last couple of days and my daughter had her bathing suit under a fleece top and leggings. For God's Grace! I give up!

I decided unless there are wind chill advisories in our area, or it's snowing or sleeting, I let them go without a coat. If they are cold, they will remember the next time on their own. I can't always be the one in charge of their choices or remembering everything for them. They need to be self-sufficient adults one day.

Thirdly, slaving over home-cooked meals *every night* is just not always feasible for a mom. I don't care if you work outside of the home, or inside of the home, or somewhere in a "she shed" in the backyard. Sometimes you just can't! Some nights a "Hot and Ready" cheese pizza from Little Caesar's is as good as it gets, or cereal and milk are just going to have to do. My kids are not going to suffer from that. In all actuality, I am just preparing them for their college and early adulthood grocery budget. Add a couple of Ramen Noodles and they will be golden. Period.

Third and a half, all those permission slips and project lists are a ridiculous waste of paper! They don't go out early enough and, if they did, your bank account is not a never-ending stream of project funds. So yeah, you will procrastinate, and sometimes that adds to the excitement. You might even get to go to the store by yourself for a quick therapeutic trip if you play your cards right.

Fourthly, having children who quietly lay their heads down to go to bed after lovingly being read to is a pipe dream. It's that simple folks. It is up there with the Easter Bunny, peeing in peace, and actually remembering to move that *stinking elf* every night!! Unless I have run them ragged taking them hiking, biking, and swimming, they are going to hop out of that bed like crickets on caffeine.

They will need drinks, and dolls, and all sorts of nonessential bedtime paraphernalia that happens to come to their little childlike minds. And even if I did run them ragged, they would probably cry incessantly because they were overtired.

There will be monsters that don't exist and stuffed animals they haven't snuggled with for at least six months that they can't sleep without.

There will be anxious nights before big baseball games or school plays. There will be sad nights because the third guinea pig died, but it was their favorite. There will be nights with tears for the dog they never met, who died before they were born, but they still miss her.

Not to mention the nights they complain of a "pushing tummy" again and just when you are ready to lose your patience, they rush to the bathroom and you realize that just maybe they weren't stalling this time.

Most nights, gritted teeth and having to threaten them with losing a privilege if I hear *one more word* is commonplace and normal mommy working conditions. Other nights, it's nurse duty, Pedialyte and sleeping on the floor of the bathroom with them.

Lastly, is it a wonder why many moms don't see clutter, crumbs, and the grimy marks? If 30 days of sleep deprivation wreaks havoc on one's verbal skills where you can't even muster the words *burp cloth*, is it any wonder what 16 years of being entrenched in the vocation would do to one's eyesight? I actually had to buy a pair of cheaters from Dollar General the other day just to start typing this book. True story!

And don't get me started on baseboards and ceiling fans. Who even looks at them? If you come to my house, look me in the eyes. I will promise they will be happy to see you. They will glisten blue and clear like freshly cleaned windows. You will see

All the Things

into my soul. Honestly, I will let you in on a little secret, my

baseboards don't talk, and my ceiling fans aren't very funny

either. But the people in my house, oh, how they will make you

laugh. You might even laugh so hard you drop some crumbs from

your mouth, and they fall on the floor. Don't worry. I will get

them another day.

3
SUPERMOMS

Superheroes have super powers. This is something that is accepted without question. Superman can fly. No problem. He can freeze things with his super breath. Got it! We don't judge him for the bright spandex he wears or question the need for a cape. It is what it is. A fashion statement and accessory.

The Flash is wicked fast. If you need a buddy to help you out, he is the one to call. He will be there before you hang up on your end. However, we don't judge him for reacting too fast. We don't chide him and ask him to think things through before reacting.

All the Things

The Hulk, well, his power is a little on the wild side, but we are fine with it. We don't recommend anger management or group therapy. We don't even judge the green color makeup he chooses to don when angry. Tame the beast? No, he is alright with us.

Spiderman, being bit by a radioactive spider, and being able to spin webs able to carry the weight of a two-ton truck? Absolutely. We don't gossip about him spinning one too many webs. We don't talk about his suit being too tight and hugging his body. We don't question his history and how he came to get his gifts. Who hasn't seen a radioactive spider? I am sure there are a few right now lurking in my basement.

Surely, we can't overlook Wonder Woman with her invisible jet and magic lasso. With nary a hair out of place, she flits from place to place taking care of bad guys with ease and beauty. We don't speak of her cleavage being a little to showy or her legs being a little too leggy. No way. You go girl. You rock that belt, matching bracelets, and headband. Those boots were made for walking all over those criminals!

Upon researching all of the above-mentioned superheroes, there is one that is missing in the annals of online superhero etymology. One whose powers out blast all others. One who, with the mere mention of their name, causes bad guys to retreat to their lairs.

They have the power of a wild beast and can harness the energy of the sun on most days. They can run lap after lap and often it seems they circle the earth with the missions they are ensnared to complete each day. They have both the ability to transform like that of the Wonder Twins and possess the strength of Superman when needed to lift the hearts, spirits, and minds of those in their charge.

Like the Flash, they are quick to react and get ALL THE THINGS done that are needed. From school, to karate lessons, to remembering the brown bagged lunch for the field trip, they have it under control. In record time they can circle the town and make all the stops.

Who is this superhero I speak of? Who has the ability of so many greats yet lacks their own comic book? It is no other than Supermom.

So here is a tribute to all the Supermoms out there.

The ones who can change out of spit up covered clothes in record time, manage to get breakfast for their kiddos, and to work on time before Clark Kent could even close the phone booth door.

The ones who can transform into nurse, teacher, preacher, judge, and jury before Spiderman's webs have thought of being spun.

The ones who handle whining, crying, stomping, biting, and spitting with ease and patience whereas the Hulk would have destroyed seven tall buildings after meltdown #1.

The ones who handle the stress of everything on their own due to singleness, military deployments, family illnesses, addiction, lack of involvement, or having been widowed. These

All the Things

Supermoms don't have the luxury of becoming invisible to escape their lives on a jet. And quite frankly, I think Wonder Woman might have hung herself with her magic lasso if she dealt with all the struggles of these Supermoms.

Supermoms are everywhere we look. However, because they don't wear a costume emblazoned with a special logo, they often go overlooked. They are invisible but not in a good way.

So, the next time you see a mom in a grocery store who is sighing and looking beaten down, just remember you wouldn't chastise Superman for being a bit too tired and needing to catch his breath having just flung a meteor back into space. Just know that she probably just got done with another round of Supermom jobs that far outweigh one meteor. She needs a smile, a pat on the back, and perhaps an encouraging word. It won't be but a matter of minutes before the Supermom emblem shines in the sky again and she is called to duty once more.

4
STICKY SITUATIONS

It is amazing the situations you find yourself in when you are a parent that you *never* thought you would be in. The words you professed would never eek from your mouth often bellow repeatedly. They are just on continual loops for our listening pleasure.

And then there are the words you absolutely never imagined would utter from your lips such as......"What is in your mouth? Come here...what is in your mouth? Is that *Super Glue in your mouth*??????" Yup. You read that right. We had quite a sticky situation in our house. The exact course of events was never completely extrapolated; however, we have come to a couple of conclusions.

One, our daughter is like a crow. She will take anything little and miniature and claim it as her own and find a home for it somewhere in her room. Her stealth like ability has this happen long before you even realize you are missing it.

Second, a tube of Super Glue Gel looks a lot like a tube of lip gloss to a two-and-a-half-year-old who wants to be a lot like mommy putting on makeup.

And three, never say *never*. I mean this in all sincerity sister. You are setting yourself up with the utterance of said word. Don't even let your mind entertain the thought. Think Harry Potter here. Just don't say it. Forever more it shall be acknowledged only as "the word that shall not be."

There are a couple of parts of this multi-act play that I must take ownership of. I can admit that yes, there was Super Glue in our kitchen. It was in our junk drawer which literally houses 9 million other items of no such risk such as instructions to

All the Things

our refrigerator, bamboo chopsticks, and many, many other non-sticky toddler-friendly items.

I also admit that yes, there was a small child who could easily get hold of it. However, we have yet to figure out how and when the small crow like girl child opened and acquired said glue. And upon closer analysis, the tube was completely brand new and had never been opened. I guess she figured that we just needed some help in that department and her teeth are pretty strong.

By the time I was notified, via screams and tears, the damage had been done. She realized this situation was not as glamorous as she thought it would be. The gloss was less glossy and a lot stickier. She needed help, and fast!

I quickly picked her up and moved into the well-lit bathroom when I realized we weren't just dealing with a minor finger pinch. She was crying, salivating, and had a whitish substance all over. It was on her hands, lips, cheeks, teeth, the roof of her mouth, and tongue.

All the Things

Evidently the sharp pearly whites of a two-and-a-half-year-old do wonders for a quick and forceful opening of a tube of Super Glue. (Take note for future encounters of such magnitude. Go right now and move your Super Glue to a top cabinet. I will wait here without judgment.)

If you can, imagine taking a white candy of Tootsie Roll consistency and stuffing about two of them in your mouth. Then allowing said candy confection to harden on your bottom teeth, you can get a vivid picture of what we were dealing with.

All the while, Sis just kept crying and saying it tasted so yucky. This was no Tootsie Roll folks. None of this was quite what she thought she was going to be experiencing at the onset of her great idea.

So, once we realized what we were dealing with I did what any good mother who lives in the age of technology does. I Googled it. I searched "Super Glue in the Mouth."

I found 1,530,000 hits in .27 seconds.

All the Things

With this result, I felt a little less freaked out, and more able to concentrate on fixing this situation my little princess had put herself in. This was not Poison Control Mode. However, other questions started darting through my mind. How could I get this off her teeth? Would it take away her enamel? Would she have a silver grill adorning her mouth for her third birthday? That was not quite the tea party theme I was going for.

The first result in our Google search was a case study about a child doing the same thing. Their solution was to use margarine because of its molecular makeup being stronger than the glue.

Wonderful. Perfect. No problem.

Then I realized that with our new "healthy living" mantra we had no margarine. It is basically plastic, so I am not feeding it to my family, and therefore I found myself back to square one.

Then I found another person who posted on Ask.com. Now mind you, this is the exact site I had just discussed with my middle school students that you *don't* use as a source for a research paper because you don't know who is posting the information and how valid it is.

At this point in our crisis, however, I pretty much ate my own words and felt if someone was reading and commenting on such a site, they probably had good cause and similar experience. So, trick number two.... Vaseline. I scurried to the bathroom cabinet in high hopes. Yes! We had it! We decided we were going to give it a whirl.

Lucky for us, the "E.R. doctor" who posted, or whoever it was, was *right*. The Vaseline helped to break down the cement-like bond. Along with the salty tears and constant rabid frothy state of Sis's mouth, I was able to get most of the glue off her lips, tongue, and teeth. Despite the concoction's positive assistance, this was no easy task.

I was literally chipping off the glue like a stone cutter with huge hunks falling out of her mouth. The roof of her mouth was a challenge, and she did have to go to bed with a slight film still on the side of her mouth. The Vaseline broke this down, eventually, but it was not pleasant.

After the crisis was averted, the discussion began. We talked about how that was very dangerous, how we don't put things in our mouth that are not food. Of course, she had no clue how horribly tragic this event could have been. The "what ifs" flew in the mind of this mother. I am thankful the worst of it was the horrible taste she had in her mouth.

Yet, one thing keeps coming back to me.

You see, she had a plan, an idea, and for the most part she thought it was going to turn out great. She got this and was going to do that. Period. End of story.

But when her plan did not turn out the way she thought it would, she found herself in quite a different situation. She could have hidden and tried to keep it from me. She could have tried to fix it herself, but this would have led to getting more things "stuck" and involved than need be.

All the Things

None of those solutions would have worked. So, she did what she felt she needed to do. She called for help. She called out to the one who she knows will drop whatever it is to come to her aid.

How many times have you found yourself in a similar situation? Maybe it didn't involve Super Glue, but it was probably very messy and sticky, and you just didn't see how you were going to get yourself out of it. Maybe you hid this situation because it was simply so embarrassing or hurtful to others that you couldn't bear to see their faces when the truth was revealed. Or, perhaps you truly couldn't get yourself out. You couldn't fix this mess on your own.

The thing is, that we *all* find ourselves in these situations. We have great ideas of certain paths, or jobs, or relationships working out. We eagerly see how it all will work out for our benefit and bless our lives and the lives of those around us. We don't always think through the exact routes of exit if things go south. We haven't Googled all the angles beforehand. We don't always want to go to "Ask.com" because quite frankly, we don't care to listen to what others have to say.

That is when we go head on into situations that were never intended for us. They looked all glossy and glamorous on the outside. Our brains were putting the puzzle together in record time, but we soon find ourselves stuck.

Perhaps we find ourselves in financial stickiness that has just added up. Maybe a medical crisis or a lost job has put you in a hole financially. Sometimes it is the spending and needing just one more thing that has gotten out of control and now burdens us and our families in ways that seem insurmountable. If you are here, call out for help. Seek financial counseling that can help you start chipping away at that debt. It is doable, albeit uncomfortable.

For others, we may suffer with fear and anxiety that makes it feel as if our mouths are sealed shut. We can't get the words out that we so desperately need to so that our truths are heard, and our hearts are healed. I tell you, call out for help.

All the Things

There are online platforms and support groups where you don't have to show your face or say a word out loud. Use these platforms as training wheels to get your confidence. Then when you are ready, start talking to real people who can help you slowly peel off the layers of Super Glue that have been keeping you stuck.

Find a trusted counselor or friend who you can start confiding in. Your words matter and they need to be spoken and heard. There is release in the speaking, and growth in the hearing. It is a symbiotic relationship between both parties.

Regardless of what you are going through, or how deep a pit you find yourself in, there is always one who is present and ready to listen. There is always one who is not too busy with other plans or situations. God is always there for his children. He knows full well the Super Glue we have in our cabinets of life. He knows our childlike ways are going to think we have it all figured out. And when we show up with tears in our eyes and frothy mouths, he is there. He doesn't have to Google or ask anyone. He knows

how to comfort us and what to do to lift our chins to him.

Psalm 120:1 says, "In my trouble I cried to the Lord, and

he answered me." When you find yourself in the darkness and

stickiness of life, cry out to God. Ask him to help you. Ask him to

start chipping away all that is burdening you down or keeping

you stuck and not able to move forward. He will surely answer

you with people in your life who will come forward with help,

support, and aid.

Now, remember how that glue tasted disgusting for little

Sis? God's not always going to send something sweet and tasty

your way. Sometimes growth and peeling of layers hurts *really*

bad! It is not comfortable.

The people he puts in your situation may not present

things the way you thought they would go. They may not say

things the way you would say them. It is not what we would have

chosen. Little Sister wouldn't have chosen to gargle with Vaseline, but it worked!!! And honestly, our ways led us to the stickiness in the first place. We need to hand over the GPS on this one.

I pray that as Sis gets older, she can still remember that regardless of the sticky situations she finds herself in, that I will always be there to help her out. But more importantly, God will never forsake her.

5
VISIONS OF PERFECTION

Whisperings. Visions. The yet to be; revealed in dreams of slumber. Inspiration arrives in the most unexpected of places. All of these have been bestowed upon me in my life. Sometimes I have brushed them off, for fear of sounding absurd. Other times I have pondered them, tried to analyze them, and discussed them openly with friends and family. I have learned over the years to embrace them. However, sometimes the inspiration seems so dreamlike and distant we are sure that is all it is. We wait and wait, and *nothing*. We become tired and testy, and the dream dies. It becomes a fading memory or wish of what might have been.

All the Things

This is a story of an inspiration. It started a strong need to complete something that was so foreign to me yet needed to be done. I had no idea what would become of it, or why I was compelled to do it. But I listened to the whisperings. I was overcome with a need to finish what I started. So, I worked diligently. I didn't stop until it was done.

It all started when my mother and I were at a store shopping together. We were browsing the card section when I saw it. Tucked in the racks of blank cards she sat quietly. A black and white card of a little girl. Her angelic profile just pulled me in and stopped me in my tracks. It was as if I knew her or had met her.

She was calling me.

Her silence begged me to take her with me, and to make her bigger than she was.

I decided I needed to buy that card. I had to draw her. I felt compelled to put her down on paper even though I had not drawn in years. Drawing had once been something that brought me so much peace and relaxation, but my life had filled up with

other things that kept me in constant motion. In addition, I would

be flying home to Illinois in a few days and I had no paper and no

pencils. However, the push and pull I felt in my heart was so

strong that I quickly went and got some supplies at a local craft

store before my flight.

Later the next day, bound for home, I had my art supplies

and little paper girl tucked into my carryon. When I left my

parents' house, my itinerary was set with only enough time to get

from my one connecting flight to my second leg home. However,

once I arrived in Pittsburg there was a problem with weather, and

I ended up having an unexpected and much longer layover which

lasted a couple of hours. Normally, I would use such time to

people watch, stretch my legs, get some coffee, and take in all that

surrounded me. However, I found myself in a faux leather seat,

with my paper girl, as the world passed us by.

I was pulled in to the photo and to this foreign little girl.

Why was she so familiar to me? Who did she remind me of? How could such a black and white profile of a small child evoke such emotion in my heart? All these questions filled my mind and I felt an awakening in my heart that I had never felt before. To be so connected to a stranger on a blank greeting card was quite odd. I know this. If I had shared my story with any of the other travelers that day, they probably would have nicely smiled, and slowly exited stage left. So, I focused on her and kept to myself which as a natural chatterbox is not normal.

However, the feelings to capture her likeness on my large 14 x 16 paper was palpable. My pencil began the dance as the graphite swooped and dipped. Slowly, her profile emerged. She was deep in thought with her fingers together in the act of praying. She was not anxious. She was focused. What was it that she was praying for? What was she talking to her Heavenly Father about?

As I continued, I focused on her eyes and hair. Her lashes were long like a deer. Wisps of hair fell across her face and I could imagine touching that soft baby-like hair. She came to life on the paper. Her angelic face and beauty were astonishing. I knew her

yet had never seen her in my life. I felt connected to her on a deep

level. This is her. We hung her in our home with a sign above her

that says, "Abide in Him."

As I said, this was in 2002. I had not given birth to any

children yet. However, I had lost a baby that spring. It was a

lonely, dark, confusing place to be. It was a secret sisterhood I had

unknowingly joined. Up until that time, miscarriage wasn't

something that was commonly spoken about. It was whispered after the fact. I could have used the rallying of my sisters who had gone down this road before. However, at that time, many were silent.

I don't judge their silence, but I feel that to value the life that was lost, I must speak my heart. To truly help others move through waters they are new to navigating, I must share that I found myself being tossed and turned in the current. Pretending my life is and always has been safe from the water's edge helps no one. Rip tides pull us away and currents pull us under.

Looking back now, I know that I was in a deep dark place. I was in a period of depression, but I didn't recognize it myself at the time. Spring ended and summer began. I had a lot of time on my hands being on a break from teaching. I tried to fill my time and focus on other things, but it didn't really work. My mind would wander away and I would find myself lost in thought. One day this happened stands out.

All the Things

I remember riding with my husband in his small black S10 truck shortly after the loss. We were driving to an event at his parents' house and the conversation we were having was not deep nor of great importance in the grand scheme of things. Suddenly, a feeling of weightlessness came over me.

I was listening to him, and could hear sound, but nothing made sense. I was riding next to him but was not physically in my body at the time. I felt as if I was floating next to my body and I could see myself sitting there. It was surreal and something I had only heard about on weird alien interview shows.

Later my husband would recognize these times. He would tell me he could tell when I was "gone." I think this was my brain trying to make sense of a senseless loss. It was my way of stopping the motion around me and resting in the silence. It was my body's way of healing from the inside and starting with my heart without the worldly distractions that I so readily would pile on.

All the Things

Many days I would look at that picture hanging on my wall and wonder. Was this a sign of the baby I was supposed to have but I had lost? Was this to tell me that I had lost a daughter? I had no idea. Yet I didn't feel sad when I looked at her. I felt at peace. An odd calming peace. So, I kept her hanging on my wall, where I could walk past her each day.

The sign above reminded me to "Abide in Him." Abide is a verb. It is in an action we do. It is defined as continuing without fading or being lost. This drawing helped me do just that. With her hanging there, the darkness slowly lightened, and I took each day one at a time.

Later that year I got pregnant again. To say I was nervous would be a grave injustice to the fear I held. I worried if I would make it past the 12-week mark, which was the death knell of my first pregnancy. I worried at each ultrasound, that the heart would be silent. The anxiety as I sat there in the dark ultrasound room each time constricted my chest like a snake. However, God placed people, physicians, and support in my life during this time. Each one helped to soften the worry a little more. The weeks plodded on and my belly continued to grow. And grow. And grow.

As I would waddle past the drawing of my little girl, I wondered if this drawing was a sign. Was I going to have a girl? We didn't find out the gender of this baby as we wanted to be surprised.

On July 15, 2003 we welcomed our oldest into our lives. We were overjoyed with a son. I was not sad that I had not had the girl in my drawing. I was at peace. An odd calming peace.

Two years later I became pregnant again. Again, I wondered, *"Could this baby be the one in the photo? Was this going to be my girl or a baby brother for our oldest?"*

The fear and worry I had experienced was less the second time around. This was probably due to having a two-year-old who still was getting up in the night, trying to potty train, and all that goes on with this age.

On April 6, 2006 we welcomed our second child to our family. A baby boy joined our family and I accepted the fact that perhaps I was going to be a mother just to sons. I was okay with that. I felt blessed that I had two healthy boys who were growing and thriving.

I was overjoyed to think of all the adventures and activities our boys would help me enjoy again. I looked forward to teaching them how to throw a baseball and ride a bike. Trains, frogs, and bugs became our new normal pastimes. Life was good. God was good.

Then a wave hit. It was a rogue one. The kind that sweeps you off your feet. Sometimes people are lost at sea from these types of waves. You might be standing there minding your own motherhood business and enjoying some Thomas the Train time. Then *boom* it hits. It completely takes you down. It fills your lungs with salty water and burns.

My wave came in the form of multiple complications from an awful gallbladder surgery when my youngest son was almost two. After surgery, I was hospitalized with numerous blood clots that were unexplainable. I was forced to be on medicine for many months and I was told by my attending physician that, "There is a very strong chance your baby bearing days are over."

When the doctor told me this, I was heartbroken. I sat bedridden in the hospital looking blankly at the walls. All I could think was, "But I'm not *done!*" I was *not* at peace. There was nothing calming in the doctor's words. It wasn't that I wanted my girl. It was just a very strong urge that I wasn't *done*. Our family was not complete. This couldn't be how it would all go down.

However, part of me felt guilty. Shouldn't I be grateful for what I have? So many women don't get the opportunity to even carry a child and here I was having a pity party for myself. But party I did. I cried. I worried. I wondered why this was happening. I questioned and questioned and questioned.

Six months later, when I was done taking blood thinners for blood clots in my legs, my doctors gave me the go ahead. With special prenatal vitamins we could try to add to our family. We decided if it was going to happen again then we would give it to

God. His plan was what we needed to cling to. I tried to remember to "abide." I continued.

Three years later when I became pregnant again, it was a completely different story. There were many doctors' appointments to make sure everything was going along in a healthy fashion. I prayed for health. I prayed for this unborn baby. I prayed for no complications. I did ALL THE THINGS the books say to do. I would like to say I took it easy and rested when I was tired, but let's all be real here. With two boys of 6 and 4 there was no rest for this go around. They were *busy*. This baby was going to have to hold on to this merry-go-round and hold on she did.

On February 1, 2010 we welcomed our daughter into our family. She was absolutely perfect in every way. Our lives were filled with newborn smells and cries. The first weeks and months flew by and we found what was a normal routine for a family of five. Two big brothers were quick to help with binkies and reading books to their little sissy.

All the Things

Soon we were carrying sissy to her brothers' hockey games. Then there were baseball games with her in the stroller watching from the sidelines. In short time, at nine months, she proceeded to learn how to walk at those baseball games and play in the dirt piles. Life with three little ones was a blur at times. It seemed to just spiral into endless days and sleeps.

However, one night, while sitting for dinner at our table, I looked up from bowing my head and there she was. At three years old, I truly saw her for who she was and who she had always been. With her head bowed, her hands folded in prayer, and her long black lashes, there she was. My whisper, my sign, my vision of perfection at His best.

Here was my angel. The one I saw so long ago. The one I was compelled to draw because I knew her. She was a part of me that had not existed yet on my timetable. She is the one who makes our lives complete, the one He told me I would have all along if I would only "Abide in Him."

All the Things

After seeing her at the dinner table, obviously without my camera at the ready, I had her pray again after dinner so I could take her picture. I could hardly believe my eyes. I had no idea I was going to write this book back then. I just needed to document this event. It was unworldly. It was odd. I knew it. It was unbelievable and things may seem embellished. I needed to take this photo so my heart could wrestle with this uncovering.

So, I ask you, what signs have you been given? Have you heeded them, or have you given up? What have you have brushed off because it didn't seem to be happening on your timetable?

All the Things

When have you been asked to continue, to abide, and you decided to just stop? How would your life look differently if you continued even when the path was unclear? How would you grow by walking in the knowledge you were covered?

What things have been whispered to you? What things came to you in odd thoughts or visions? What have you been pulled to that you cannot explain in this world? What dreams have you had that you let die because you thought they were too far-fetched?

My words to you are simple. Be patient and faithful my friend. Believe. Hang that sign where you can see it every day.

Simply "Abide in Him" and his artwork unfolding will amaze you.

6
PUPPY LOVE

We have a dog. He is soft. He is cuddly. He doesn't shed. My children love him. They wanted him. They begged for him. I see the joy in their eyes. The love that flows, when they interact with him in their own individual ways, makes my heart smile.

I know it was God's plan to have him join our family. It was the right time and he was the right dog. I love him! We all do. Even the hubby who tries to deny it has been heard uttering baby talk to him. This dog is irresistible. His name is Hardson, but we called him Hardy. He is a preloved dog that found his way into our lives via a friend who had a new baby.

All the Things

Here is the kicker. I also know he will break our hearts one day. That little girl who is smiling so wide in the picture, will grieve and her cheeks will be streaked with tears that I cannot stop. The joy they have for him now, will lead to sadness. There is no way to avoid this. As my husband pointed out recently, "All relationships will end one day."

I guess there was one way we could have sheltered our children from such sadness. We could have totally avoided the whole situation. We could have remained in the petless population that many families choose. It is easier that way.

If we don't love, we don't hurt. But then again, are we really living? Are we experiencing the life we are gifted with, or merely existing? Are we preparing our children for life?

In the last year, the feeling of loss has crept into my everyday life. From events of the world, to events in our family, my heart has hurt. My chest has felt heavy and I have had days that tears have streaked my face. My once happy smile has been absent. My patience has been tested and my temper has flared.

My thoughts have been swimming in loss. The loss of ones so young and in the prime of their lives. The loss of friends who were the fabric of my entire adult life. The loss of battles fought long and hard. Battles that had unfairly been handed to them and not to others.

I have wanted to seek out a cave. I have wanted to roll the rock closed and just be alone. I want to see nothing. I don't want the light to filter in because its images are too overwhelming. I don't want to hear anymore because the sounds are too deafening.

I think of other cave dwellers. For I am not alone. There are many

reasons we want to retreat.

For some, they have seen such beauty and brilliance, and

then it was snatched away. The beauty around them was

impressive, and fantastic. It was full of life and vitality. But now

that it is gone it is too painful to look at anything. For nothing will

replace that loss. For them, the cave is a safe place. For them, they

cannot and will not allow themselves the pain of looking at the

light again. Their heart will remain guarded and under

permanent lock and key.

And then I think about life outside that cave. The life we

live. The life that has both beauty and brutality. This is the life that

both pulls and pushes us along when we feel we cannot go on

anymore. This is the life my children live in and will grow up in.

Walking children through grief is not found in the

manuals when you get the early pregnancy books. We cannot

prepare for that part of the journey because each child, each individual heart will deal with loss differently.

I cannot keep them from loving and losing any more than I can stop the air from blowing. It is part of their journey. It is part of my journey. It is how we grow and learn to give. To give of things and more importantly of ourselves.

As a parent, I have found loving my children is the easiest and scariest thing I have ever done. I am not saying parenting is easy. Please hear me clearly. For the love of *God*, it is the hardest thing I have ever done! But loving them and truly getting to know each of them for the sacred creation of God that they are, is easy. But from the moment I brought them into this world, knowing that they could be gone from my world is the scariest thing to live with each day.

But do I crawl into the cave because it could happen? Did I choose not to be a parent because the prospect of the pain of loss was too much? No. The daily brilliance far outweighs the possibility of the pain.

All the Things

The laughter and smiles take away the fear of the unknown. Experiencing their love and lives overshadows the what ifs. It is more powerful than the darkness. They are the light. They must be.

If I live my life protecting myself from the light, then I never see the brilliance. If I always worry about being hurt and losing what I love, then I have already lost it. I will miss out on meeting the colorful people who will fill my heart with joy.

I will never hear their stories that both break my heart and mend it all at the same time. If I live my life excluding the difficult things we hear, I also don't hear the words that will heal my heart or inspire me to inspire others.

It can't work both ways. We can't both live in darkness and shine light at the same time. Once again, I choose the light and a puppy who for now, is bright white and full of life. A life we are enjoying regardless of what tomorrow may bring.

And when "tomorrow" comes, whenever that day is, we will take our children's tender hearts and hold them gently and help them to grieve. It is a lesson. A lesson we all will have

multiple times in our lives.

But today, we play. Today we laugh. Today we snuggle

and cuddle a fluffy puppy we are blessed to call our own.

7
BUILDING WITH DIRECTION

When my boys were between the ages of five and ten, they went through what I will refer to as the "Lego" stage. This stage was a unique stage unlike the "Thomas the Train" stage from the age of two. With Thomas they would play for hours on the floor making new track layouts and creating scenarios. Thomas and his friends were quite the problem solvers. The Lego stage was entirely different.

No, this one was more of a stage rooted in the visual appeal of all that Lego had to offer. We would peruse the aisles of Walmart looking for birthday gifts for friends, or to kill time while getting our oil changed, and there they would be. Boxes and boxes of new and creative, colorful plastic bricks would be from the floor to the ceiling. The sweet Danish bricks beckoned my boys with their siren songs.

Then the words would begin.

"Mom this one would go perfectly with the X fighter I got for my birthday. Look at this cool one!"

"Uh huh," was my reply.

They would ooh and aah over the various magical sets that went with the newest Harry Potter movie.

"Mom, look, this one has Hagrid! That is awesome," they would continue.

"Yup, pretty neat," I would add while *not* making eye contact.

It is important to note that when navigating the toy aisle, you avoid at all costs looking directly into their eyes. Their eyes would light up and they would talk about how cool these were. They possess a quality much like that of Kaa, the snake, from the

Jungle Book. Look down sister. Look up. Just don't look directly

into them until you have formulated a *"hard no"* in your mind.

They would continue how these new ones were so much

better than the other ones they had at home. I could see the

enthusiasm rushing through their veins with all the possibilities of

hours of independent and creative play.

The excitement was invigorating, but as usual we would

leave the store void of those colorful boxes. I avoided their direct

eye contact and pushed through the aisle with my ATM card

unscathed.

I could hear them in the minivan on the ride home. They

would be mumbling under their breath how I was such a mean

mom. "What are you talking about back there?" I would ask.

"Nothing," they would counter with downtrodden voices.

Yup. I would hear them agree that I never got them anything fun

when we went to the store. Yup.

All the Things

This would continue until we got home, and they moved

on to playing with something else or got distracted by any

number of other items that already lived in our house.

Months later, when friends and family would ask us for

ideas regarding what our boys would like for their birthdays or

Christmas, I would tell them about the various Lego sets they had

seen. The parties or celebrations would arrive, and my boys

would squeal with delight at their new boxes of colorful bricks.

They could barely contain their excitement to open the

boxes. They would scurry to any open spot in the house and

proceed to rip open said box. I would encourage them to pick a

spot where they could spread out and see all the pieces, to make

sure they had enough room to open them up so they could follow

the books of instructions to create their masterpieces. They would

oblige and the hours of fun would begin.

These times of fun would usually have times of frustration

when they needed the guidance of either my husband or myself.

They would have a hard time managing to read the instructions or find the piece that would fit perfectly. Upon closer examination, rereading the directions, and having someone with a different perspective, they would usually change their attitude and continue with their construction projects.

When their "star fighters" were finished or their latest castles were standing tall, the play would begin. Even though I would tell them to put the directions in a safe place for future use, they would always be inadvertently misplaced and never found again. Then they would take their masterpieces into their rooms.

Days later, when the excitement and newness had waned, I would find them once again in their rooms. They would tell me they were bored. They had nothing to do. They had nothing to play with. Their motivation and creativity had peaked and fallen.

I would encourage them to play with their Legos. I would ask them where their "star fighter" was. Where did you put Hagrid's castle? I would scan their room to no avail.

"We took it apart," they would respond.

"Why?" I would ask.

"We wanted to make something different. We got tired of playing with them, so we made new stuff."

"Oh, okay. That makes sense. Well, do you want to play with the "star fighter" again?"

"Yeah, but it is too hard," they would answer.

"What is hard about it? You made it before," I would tell them.

"Well, the thing is mom. We can't find the directions. We lost them. Our pieces are all in different places. We can't remember how to make it the right way. It keeps coming out wrong. No matter how hard we try, it just keeps messing up."

So, I did what any good mother with access to Pinterest would do. I looked at how to organize their Legos in such a fashion that it would be easier for them to access them. I spent way too much on plastic bins and tubs. I spent hours on their bedroom floor crippling my legs.

At first, they were there helping. They were excited about the idea of having things more organized. Then the hours turned to half a day, and those same boys were long gone. The noontime sun turned amber in the sky and soon stars were above.

However, I had completed the task! There were bins for the red, yellow, white, gray, black, and green bricks. There were bins for the really large pieces and ones for the very small people, tires, wings, engines, and weapons. There were even bins for a couple of the directions that were pulled from under their beds or behind their dressers. It was all color coded and ready for their hot little hands to explore.

This was going to be awesome!!!!

Until it wasn't.

Guess what? They still were frustrated that they couldn't put their old pieces back together the way they used to be. Their color-coded brick tubs became a kaleidoscope of plastic in record time. My whole day of organizing, searching, and making things easier for them was for naught. They weren't using the system the way I had it set up. They were still doing things their way and finding it frustrating.

All the Things

How often do we find ourselves in the same situations in our lives? No, we are not perusing the aisles for Legos, but instead we walk the maze of IKEA. We scan the pictures on Pinterest of things we don't have. We see things that could adorn our house. The new things would go just right with what we already have, but just a tad bit better.

We are always on the lookout for the next best thing. We tell ourselves this will make us happy. This will give us contentment. This will make things better and more exciting. The world constantly bombards us with this lie and we continue to lap it up like newborn kittens with warm sweet milk. It fills our bellies and makes us "milk drunk."

Then one day, we are surprised when the "thing" we were wanting lands in our lap. Something is given to us. It is a gift wrapped up in the perfect box of love, compassion, and grace. Perhaps it is in the form of a new job, a new relationship, a new house, or a new child. This is what we have been waiting for. This time it is going to be different. We are going to cherish this gift.

All the Things

We know God tells us how to live our lives. He has left us His word so our lives may be rich and filled with all we need. In Psalm 32:8 God tells us, "I will show you and teach you in the way you should go. I will tell you what to do with my eye upon you."

So, we do what we know we need to do.

We follow the instructions.

We make sure to read all the directions. Once. Twice. Three times we review them and make sure all the steps are checked off. We see what the outcome of our hard work and the gift looks like. We are happy with ourselves. We sit back and take it all in. GOD is so good.

We tell ourselves this time will be different. We will stay true to his directions. But then our childlike ways swoop right in. We toss God's words aside. We don't think we need them right now. We are just going to tweak things a little bit.

We have some ideas and they sound exciting. His directions become misplaced. We are having so much fun taking the gift and making it into what we want it to be. We take apart all that He has instructed us to do. Brick by brick the deconstruction happens, and other people join in too. They see this frenzy of creativity and they want to join us. It looks so fun.

Together we look at all the endless possibilities. We talk and hold conferences. Surely, we can make something better. We have the brains and capabilities to modify the design and make it more creative. We think about how we can repurpose pieces and make things multi-functional. We can create bricks that are better for the planet, for the world, for its people.

However, when we are working so hard at "our vision" we often venture forward trying to fashion new bricks together that are not well built. We create designs that were never intended to hold the weight of the world. When these "original designs" we have fashioned fail, and they often do, we get frustrated.

We lash out at each other. We are again children who are throwing up our hands.

All the Things

We ask why our "star fighter" just doesn't seem to look or fly right. We feel defeated when the castle we have built on our own seems less magical than the architectural plans had seemed. Everything is off kilter.

Sometimes, many times, we get angry with God. Why did he give us such a gift and then let it turn out this way? It wasn't supposed to be this way. This is not how the box looked when we were pining for it.

However, the problem is we have lost the true nature and purpose of the gift. The gift was given to us as a learning experience. It came with directions, but we were too good to follow or keep them.

Friends, we have all been there. With tears in our eyes we ask why our marriages are struggling. Why does it have to be this hard? Why can't we figure out what we want to be when we grow up? Why do we keep getting let go despite putting all our energy into that new job? Why can't our children act respectfully and not like crazed feral cats? Why did our business fail when it was the dream we had held for so long?

We all have stories to tell and examples of when our Legoland creations came tumbling down. When what we created was so off kilter it was dizzying. The key is, we need to search for those directions again. Ours aren't under our beds or behind our dressers. They are found in God's word to us in the holy book of directions he left us, The Bible. It is all there.

So, take apart your creations. Go get some bins. Reorganize your blocks. Color code them and get a label maker if you need one. Start again fresh tomorrow with the rising of the sun. Reread those directions. Create something beautiful and made to last. His directions really are foolproof.

8
BATTER UP

In my pre-parenthood days, there was a lot of advice that was given freely from many sources. Some of it was appreciated. Some of it was filed away. However, many times I just naively rolled my eyes and swore I wouldn't be *"that"* parent.

Looking back, having sixteen parenting years under my belt, it seems that much of that advice revolved around adjusting to having a baby, the months after the baby arrives, how to lose the baby weight, and how to juggle all the newness and nerve-wracking events all rolled into one. This can be a very messy time for sure.

All the Things

But where I sit now, there is much more that I would have liked to know about before getting into this profession called parenting, and I mean that with all sincerity. In fact, there is not much in terms of job experience that has gone undone in the last ten years.

I have wiped, changed, and cleaned every person, pet, and surface in this house. But that is not the hardest part of this profession. I feel the messiest part is the new chapter my children and I are entering.

You see, when babies are born, we coo over them. We snuggle them and make promises to keep them safe and secure. We cheer their first steps. We take note of their first words. When they mark these milestones, we smile, and our hearts burst with pride.

Then they learn to run, skip, ride a bike, and roller blade. There is nothing they can't do. We see their wings fluttering and we know they are going to take off.

All the Things

But some of our children battle oppressors we weren't prepared to face. There was no advice given for when your son, at eight, bursts into tears at the mere mention of playing baseball.

"MOM!!! Why did you sign me up for baseball? I don't want to play. I hate baseball!"

"No, you don't. You played it last year and liked it."

"NO, I DIDN'T! I hate it. It's boring. Why did you sign me up? I don't want to play."

(Imagine, if you will, this last line being said behind tear brimmed eyes, which are surrounded by bright red cheeks. I know. He's good at bringing the guilt.)

So, what's a mom to do? Do I become *"that"* mom? The one who forces her child to play a game because all the other kids are playing it?

No, what I do is drop the subject for the moment, hope the boy child calms down and comes to his senses. We have a long line of Yankee and Cardinal fans in our lineage.

All the Things

Later that night, I sweetly bring up this "boring baseball" issue during the nighttime ritual of tuck-in and snuggling. Surely a snuggle will make it all better.

"Honey, let's talk about baseball."

Even before the second syllable falls from my lips, tears instantly appear in the boy child's eyes and stream down his little face.

"MOM! I told you I don't want to play baseball! Why did you sign me up? You know I don't like baseball!"

And there we have it! He is not budging.

"But why? What is it about baseball that you don't like?" And that is when he falters. He looks at me with those teary eyes and decides to bare his heart.

"You want to know. You really want to know why I don't like baseball? It's because.... I'm scared. I'm scared of people looking at me. I'm scared of people laughing at me when I strike out."

All the Things

And in that moment, all I can think of is how brave my little man is to be telling the truth. How smart he is for naming why it is that he doesn't want to play baseball.

But I also want to scream, "HELLO?????? Where is the advice fountain now?"

Where are all those other mothers who so graciously told me when to stop nursing, or when to introduce rice cereal, or when to take away the sippy cup?

Those advice givers gave freely then. But helping navigate those daily messes are a breeze. What about the emotional messes? Where are the chapters and outlines to navigate those times? What wise words are we given? Where are the battle plans to slay these dragons?

Nope. Crickets. That's what most of us find.

We are forced to forge our own swords and prepare for battle the best way we know how.

I was at a loss for my little man. I sat there thinking about the two choices. Do I let him quit or do I make him play? Do I force him into something he clearly doesn't want to do, or do I help him battle this dragon known as *fear*?

I chose to help him step up to the plate.

You see, if he had told me he would rather play basketball, or paint, or take ballet, I would have been fine with it. It didn't matter that it was baseball. What mattered was that it was *fear* that was dictating his decision.

It was fear that was looking him in the face, intimidating him, and breathing dragon breath down his neck. It was fear that was holding him back from experiencing what baseball really could be. I couldn't stand by and let fear win.

So, we talked about fear. We talked about how we all have it. I talked about how I was afraid to be a mom for the first time. But I also told him that I spent time talking to other moms and reading about being a mom. I practiced taking care of other people's kids. I got all the baby gear I needed to be prepared and by the time his brother was born I felt ready. However, that didn't mean I wasn't scared at other times.

All the Things

I also mentioned that I am sure people still laugh at me in the grocery store with all three kids in tow. I have learned to ignore them and move on. Nobody has time for that. Let judgers judge. Momma's got shopping to do! She's got bellies to feed.

He smiled and laughed. I smiled and laughed and at the end of the night he decided he would at least go to practice but he wasn't "versing" anyone in a game. I decided that was progress and we could work with that.

The next day, we while we put on his cleats for practice, we realized said cleats were a little too tight. We are truth tellers here, so I will admit procrastination is an art I am honing rather than a negative quality I am afraid to admit to.

So, off we went to the most expensive sporting goods store in town because a) I knew it was the only place that would probably not be picked over, and b) it was exactly 40 minutes before practice was to start. We like to live on the edge, us procrastinators. It makes the ride a little more exciting.

All the Things

When we walked into the store, this small boy child was overcome with all the cool gear. He saw the shining helmets which would protect his head. He saw the soft leather gloves that would give him a better grip, and his feet felt the strong molded cleats that would give him traction to race down the first base line.

"Mom, these gloves feel really good on my hands......Mom, these cleats feel great on my feet......Mom this helmet fits my head perfectly."

Folks, I am not above bribing.

But more than that, I think that for many of us, when we are faced with the scary and messy parts of our lives, having the right gear makes everything seem so much easier to bear. It makes stepping up to the plate that much less intimidating and smacking the crap out of *fear* that much sweeter.

We all know fear. We all have times it whispers in our ears that we aren't good enough, strong enough, wise enough, or whatever enough. God knew we would feel this way, and he has given us the best armor for that. We don't even have to go to an

expensive store in town.

In Ephesians 6:10-17, God tells us just what we need to do

to prepare ourselves for this battle. He doesn't say some of us will

face it and others won't. We all will. Because he knows us and our

hearts so well, he tells us exactly what to wear to prepare for

battle.

"Finally, be strong in the Lord and in his mighty power.

Put on the *full armor of God*, so that you can take your stand

against the devil's schemes. For our struggle is not against flesh

and blood, but against the rulers, against the authorities, against

the powers of this dark world and against the spiritual forces of

evil in the heavenly realms. Therefore, *put on the full armor of God*,

so that when the day of evil comes, you may be able to stand your

ground, and after you have done everything, to stand. Stand firm

then, *with the belt of truth buckled around your waist*, with *the

breastplate of righteousness in place*, and with your *feet fitted with the

readiness that comes from the gospel of peace*. In addition to all this, *take up the shield of faith,* with which you can extinguish all the

flaming arrows of the evil one. Take the helmet of salvation and

the sword of the Spirit, which is the word of God."

So dear sisters, armor up. Be prepared to step up to the

plate of life and swing away!

9
THE TRUTH-TELLER CLUB

Images, perspectives, preconceived notions, wishful thinking, pride, and public scrutiny. What do all these things have in common? What do all these mean for most mothers? These are the undercurrents to how most of us choose to live our lives. These are the tides and torrents that shift the sand beneath our feet or pull our lives into chaos.

They are the images not of what is truly going on within, but what we want others to think is truth. The vivid snapshots of greatness versus the grainy ones of defeat. Those that hang proudly on our walls versus the ones we often quickly delete.

In the last few years, I have seen many friends struggle. I have struggled. We have struggled silently, publicly, quietly, and oftentimes without the knowledge of those closest to us. Other times we confide in our careful few. The ones we know won't judge or try to fix what is going on. They just listen.

The thing that has kept me thinking is what about those mothers who don't have those chosen careful few in which to trust? What if the person we see at the park, who is struggling silently with some aspect of motherhood, won't hear anything truthful from anyone else but us? However, when we get the opportunity, we remain silent.

What about the mothers we encounter who are *so* not like us in their outward appearance, yet *so* like us in their motherhood situation? How would our lives and their lives be bettered if we reached out and embraced the struggles of motherhood we all are facing?

What if we skipped the pleasantries and went straight to the white elephant in the room? What would happen if we chose to live openly and honestly, and allowed all people who know us and meet us to see all the images of us? What would that mean for the relationship of women in our lives? What would that mean

for the old stay-at-home mom vs. working mom debate that has

plagued our generation?

Honestly, would you think badly of me if you knew I

popped handfuls of M & M's at night when I was dealing with a

two-year-old who *would not go to bed*!!!! Sometimes they were

followed by a Riesling chaser! Does that make me a bad mother?

Does that make me weak?

What about the day my youngest son was laced up and

ready to take the rink for his first hockey game? How would you

have reacted seeing my blood beginning to boil when he didn't

want to get on the roller rink despite the fact he had skated since

he was three?

My patience was thin. The image of my face, when I told

him to get on that rink, was one I wish I could delete from his

memory bank. There was absolutely no image of greatness there.

Here is the thing, and in case you haven't figured it out

yet, I will let you in on the secret. None of us is perfect. Not one.

All the Things

We know that for sure. That is not debatable unless we are using huge doses of sarcasm. Yet so many times, with so many people, we choose to make it look like we are doing great! And what is that really doing for many of us women?

How does it help others to have them think we are managing to spin the 75 proverbial plates above our heads? All it does is set up the next mother or friend to think they are less than. Surely since they can't do it all, there must be something wrong with them. Right?

Wrong!

So, here is the challenge I am giving myself and I throw out to you, my beloved readers, mothers, and friends. What if for the next year we choose to live openly and honestly with all who enter our lives? Regardless of whether or not we think they will judge us, what if we show up with transparency?

What if we decide to not care about being judged? What if we just share our struggles so that other mothers will understand they are not alone. So, let's talk openly about when we resorted to punching a pillow and screaming into it because our toddler wouldn't go to sleep and we were exhausted. From today forward let these honest truths about motherhood fall from our lips. Because when we share how we don't know how to navigate this neck of the rapids, other moms will show us the way around those rocks.

On the days, when we are so tired of listening to our children bicker or physically fight with each other, we will share how our children drain us. We will share the desperation of our words not being heard and the heartbreak we feel when they treat each other so unkindly. From today on, we will be honest and tell other mommas that we feel like a failure.

When we do this, we will experience the bond and the release that so many of us need. We will feel the bonding of our experiences to others and we will feel the release of not having to feel we always have it all together. When other mommas share their journeys, they will remind us we are not failures and our stories will do the same for their hearts.

All the Things

This sharing of our hearts will help feed our souls with what we are all longing for---true connection. We are all perfectly imperfect parents raising perfectly imperfect children, in an equally imperfect world.

At my core, I believe there will be many more mothers out there who will be thankful for honesty than there will be the judgers, but even they may gain a thing or two. It might be exactly what they need to break free from the veil of make-believe. We all know the true reason people point the fingers of judgment on others is because they don't want to look carefully at their own plates. You know, the plates spinning, dropping, and crashing around them. It is a crazy circus of brokenness my friend.

So today starts day one. For the next year, let's choose to live each day with purpose, and live honestly and truthfully with the women in our lives. We will be equally honest with those who we know well, and those who we will meet. This goes for those who are in my life for the duration, and those who are only passersby. Those whose names are written on my heart and those whose names I will never know.

We have but one time around this track of life. I want to run hard and fast. I want to run with purpose and integrity. I want to run with others who can lift me up, but I also want to be one who is relied upon and trusted for honesty, transparency, and truth.

Okay, if we are being honest, I like walking much better. Running is so overrated, and I hate wearing a sports bra or two. When I think about it, and I am totally transparent, strolling is more my speed.

Let's stroll along together. It's slower, better for our joints, and we will see more beauty along the way. I don't think I will need an oxygen rest station with strolling either. Do you have other sisters who need to join us? Bring them along. There is joy in numbers.

10
A WOMAN I KNOW

There is a woman I know. She often speaks about her children and all the funny things they say and do. She recalls their stories and funny adventures to others and is so animated with her recollections of the antics of her little ones. She shares the funny ways they say words or phrases. A three-year-old saying *"guh-nana"* for *"banana"* is simply adorable.

They are truly the best and most wonderful gifts she ever received. This I know to be true. You can see the love and devotion run through her veins and bubble out of her sparkling eyes. The sun is shining brightly, and all is well in her world. Her voice has a heightened uptick and her audience can't help but be swept up in her conversations when she talks about her children and their accomplishments. She is not bragging. It is just that she is ever so proud.

However, then the darkness comes. I see her lose her patience with those same children she claims to love. Her voice becomes harsh and quick and her eyes pulse with irritation. She slays those same children with words of anger that slice and wound their tender hearts. Those words would never make it on her social media feed, and those eyes wouldn't be uploaded as her new profile pic.

When the darkness eclipses the light, she feels such shame and sadness. She knows full well the eyes of judgment are on her. When she does this, a piece of my heart breaks for her. I know later she will feel the guilt only a mother knows.

There is another woman I know. She reads things in books and can't wait to share them with others. She is a dreamer and an artist. Her mind is ever racing with new projects and creative maps line her heart. She loves to sit with tea and lose herself while painting and writing for hours. Stories fill her head but there is no time to jot them down before another one pops in its place. She

sees faces and animals in clouds and tells funny stories to her kids

at bedtime.

She watches documentaries about faraway lands and

people she hasn't met, and they root themselves into her heart.

She feels aortic tugs when she learns about children suffering and

shares these stories with her own children. She doesn't shy away

from sharing the truth of the unfairness in life and the harsh

reality of death.

There are photos on her fridge of children throughout the

world. She wants her kids to know they must always look to help

others. She encourages her family to sponsor these children and

pray for them. She talks about the need for her children to

understand their place in life is connected to others regardless of

social status or location. That together we are stronger. That

together we are smarter. That regardless of our location or level of

education, the love of our Heavenly Father is the same for all of

us.

All the Things

She navigates this world we live in with a perception of needing to help. She encourages her children to look at the world through the lens of servanthood. How can they help their neighbor? What gifts and talents have they to offer the world? With youthfulness and ingenuity on their side, how can they better the world they live in?

When I hear her talk to her children, I become inspired. I want to sit at her feet and learn how to do great things in the world. I want to take off the jaded lenses I often put on before my feet hit the floor in the morning. I want to be more like her. I want to ask her how I can help. I want her to tuck me in and tell me fantastic tales of clouds that look like whales, and ways that I can make the world a better place no matter how small I feel.

There is a friend I have. I work with her closely. We sit side by side, day in and day out. She puts on a happy face and smiles to those she sees in passing. She values her job and wants to do it well. After all, this is the job she has always wanted, and the location of the job is what she waited for. She put years in at other places, but now she is right where she always said would be her dream job.

But at the end of the day, and sometimes even at the beginning, I see in her eyes that she is tired. She is done. She is ready for the day to end, even when it is only 10:30 a.m. She is checking off the boxes and doing ALL THE THINGS. She is going through the motions. A carefully choreographed routine that has been years in the making.

But then I see her close her tired eyes. She takes a breath. And then another. They are deep yoga worthy breaths. The kind of breathing that brings dead things back to life. She takes another one and then lets out a mighty sigh of gratefulness. She pours another iced coffee, stands a little taller, and soldiers on. I see her, although she doesn't know I am watching. She makes me want to work harder.

There is a girl I know. She is filled with happiness and energy. She is the perfect recipe of equal parts Mary Poppins, Woodland Fairies, and Willy Wonka, with a dash of unicorn dust.

All the Things

When she comes to my house, she dances around the kitchen with my children like a whirling dervish. She turns the music up so loud the bass reverberates in her hips.

She picks up my daughter and spins her around and around to the tune of innocent giggles and high-pitched squeals. She is one-part ballerina and one-part interpretive dancer that cares not what the critics say. She makes up silly moves to the music and dances along with my teenage son. He would never tell her, but he likes her silliness and carefree spirit. So, do I.

She allows my middle son to climb upon her lap even though his body is more like a giant daddy long-legs spider trying to fit in a thimble. She lets him sit, and rock, and they whisper in silly voices and secret words that wouldn't make sense to anyone else. When I see the happiness on her face, and the faces of my children, I wish she would stay. I know that for the length of that song, they are carefree and making memories. For the length of that rocking chair time her time is his. There are no other distractions and for all the outside world knows, she and my children don't exist. They are in another time continuum and the outside forces cannot penetrate what she has with them. She is in love with them, and them with her.

There is a middle-aged woman I know. She is not sure where the time has gone. She pours over National Geographic articles and photos wondering what life would be like if she could visit all the beautiful and terrible places in the world. Would she have a deeper appreciation for what she has? Would she find a higher purpose? Is she doing enough with her life? What does it mean to *"do enough?"* How do we measure *"enough?"* Can she find a cup big enough? Do they sell them at HomeGoods? They have ALL THE THINGS there. She asks me if she needs to go away to find her way back. Or is she already away and needs to come back? How does one do that? Where are the atlases for that journey? I dream with this woman and listen quietly to her questions.

Another friend I know plans great things for her children to do and see and learn. When she is around, she is always teaching and talking. Her brain is always one step ahead and thinking about the next big thing they can explore. She carefully chooses her words and explains things to them.

She is the model of patience and calmness. Her words are filled with tenderness and truth. Her children are inquisitive and energetic. She keeps up with them bounding and playing, hiking and climbing. Bike rides with her are filled with conversations about turtles, how they hatch, and why wild creatures deserve to be wild.

Her children long for this time with her and I also see that she thoroughly enjoys her time with them very much. It is a mutual time of healing and connection. I long to spend more time with this friend and have every day be like a trip to the Botanical Gardens. I want her to teach me about wild things and how they long to be free.

There is another woman I know. She is always looking to improve herself. She finds inspirational quotes that she prints off and puts in little frames around her house. She finds new apps to make her life easier or her workout routines more efficient. She does her research and tries her best to do what is right for her children. She has numerous boards with the latest and greatest of menus to nourish her brood. She pins various ways to purge, clean, and organize her house.

I wish I could live in her Pinterest world. Everything would be so neat and clean, and fresh. Everyone would be so healthy and fit. Nary a thing would be out of place. Paint would always be fresh and there would always be fresh flowers through her house.

There is another friend I have. She looks around her house at her laundry piling up. How did two loads turn into three? The mismatched socks are multiplying like rabbits. The dust on the piano looks like an urn was toppled. The greasy hair of her dirty children can stand up without the need of expensive hair products. Everyone needs a good scrub including the tub after she's done with the children and herself. Is there any shampoo left or does that need to be added to the grocery list? The homework, reading logs, school projects, and permission slips line her

counter.

She wonders *"Is this it?"*

She asks me, "Is this my life?"

And I remind her this is just a phase. This is just a step. It

is a season she is weathering. This is not who you are. The is

merely where you are right now.

She listens, but I know she doesn't always believe me.

You see, there is also an old lady who visits me. She is wise

and caring, but she is often tired. Her eyes sparkle, but just a little

less than ten years ago. Her sighs tell me she is easier exasperated

than in her earlier years. She knows what needs to be done, but

often looks at things and says, "What does it really matter in the

grand scheme of things my girl? The laundry can wait. It will

always be there. Something will always be dirty. Something will

always be on the list." I often think I should listen to her more.

Her gray hairs tell me she might know a thing or two.

All the Things

These women. These women I know. I know them intimately. I know them dearly. Their lives are wrapped tightly to mine. When they laugh, I laugh. When they cry, I cry. When they lose sleep from worry and regret, I do too. I call them friends, but really, I should just call them what they really are....me.

The pieces of me all fit together to make me who I am. And all your pieces make you the beautiful mosaic of a momma that you are. All the fears and failures, the fabulous days and frustrating hours. Our finest attempts and our biggest flops. Our proudest moments and the ones we wish we could wipe away forever. They all are part of our journey.

When you feel you are being looked at with the eyes of judgment, know you are not alone. We **all** give the cashiers at Walmart and Target much to talk about on their lunch breaks. There should be some kind of discount coupon code or Krazy Kid App that they can scan for you. Honestly! Why isn't that a **thing**?

Until then, remember, when you hear that song that makes your heart sing, turn it up. Let your hips move, dance the silly dances, embarrass your teenagers, pick up your babies and make them squeal. Let those memories fill your heart. You will need to remember that sweet music when they are too big for your lap, too old to hold your hand in the grocery store, or too far away for you to see their faces in person. These precious memories of time are ALL THE THINGS that matter the most.

11
YOUR VOICE

This year marks number 23 of my teaching career. I can't believe it has been so long since I first stepped into a classroom of my own. I remember how nervous I was being hired on the night before school started. It seems like so long ago, yet in many regards it is still so fresh and new. Classrooms and situations have changed over the years which brings newness. But honestly, the beginning of school jitters and anxiety are still there. The only thing that has changed is my location.

My classroom looks a lot different than it did in years past. For the first 16 years I taught middle school in the local school district and then I took a new path and started a Montessori

All the Things

Adolescent Program. After that program ended, I decided to homeschool my own children. This year will be our second-year homeschooling and it is a constant state of learning the ropes and assessing the best course of action and needs of my students.

I still have sleepless nights before starting a new school year despite the many years on this journey. I am sure it is due to my mind reeling with what I want this year to look like and what learning strategies will suit the varying needs of my children? How can they become more independent and explore their interests while still covering all the material that will help them move forward in the coming years? What do I want to accomplish? How can I inspire my children and not strangle them at the same time? The answer to this one is to walk away. Just do it. Walk away and go get a cup of cold brew, or two.

Before I know it, our school room is ready. The physical needs are always met with a few days of prepping and help from the children. We cull the unneeded and focus on what is truly important. The maps of the world are pinned on the bulletin boards and the books are neatly on the bookshelf, for now. The walls are ready for the work my children will research and create. The walls are waiting to be covered in things far more colorful and creative than bulletin board paper.

You see, my love is writing. I know, shocking I am sure. I will pause for you to catch your breath...

Each year as new students used to enter my room, I tried to encourage them to find something they had never experienced. I asked them to discover facets about themselves they didn't know even existed. I implored them to ponder about and express their thoughts differently than many had ever been asked to do. As the years went on, I helped them to carve out their voice. A voice that so desperately wants to be heard but is often overlooked because of their age and our society.

In a world so filled with the written word being texted, tweeted, and splashed across every major news outlet, many students don't know how to voice how they really feel about things that matter. They barely know how to tread water in the world of words to express things that perhaps have grieved them

for some time. They can talk, sure, but they often struggle to write.

To get down on paper an essay, they are often filled with shock

and fear. Their bodies get fidgety and their minds wander. They

sometimes have an overwhelming urge to use the restroom....

often. These are what the students usually feel.

For some this was not the case. They were already

accomplished writers by the time I met them. Those for whom

writing came easy are like those students who teach themselves

how to play the guitar on their own. I have taught those children,

but they are a select few.

Instead, I would find my classroom filled with students

who participated in every known extracurricular activity but

couldn't write a complete sentence about what they did. They

knew how to tell their families and friends what they were

thinking, but writing such information was often a much more

difficult task.

All the Things

Even for my own flesh and blood children, putting pen to paper seems an insurmountable task. It is too hard, and they don't know where to start. So that is where I come in. That is what I love. Taking those students who *hate* to write and having them realize writing is just like talking. I actually used to even ask them, "How many of you *hate* to write?"

If I asked my own three, all of them would cheer in unison. How lucky I am. A trifecta of language haters.

When the hands would timidly find themselves in the air I would triumphantly reply, "Yes!!! We are going to have fun this year!"

They were often shocked at this response and some wryly smiled and realized I was not like the rest.

And that is how I work with my own children. We do things differently in our school. It is one of the lovely facets of homeschooling. We learn how to be writers. We become writers who can tell a story or ask a question. They are working on becoming writers who are proud of what they create regardless of the length of their written work or prior ability. We all learn at our

own pace and writing ability, and we celebrate those

accomplishments.

We write songs, stories, letters, and articles. We research

things that interest us and read other authors' styles. We write to

authors about the books they have written and ask them why they

did what they did in the hopes of helping us to be better writers in

the future. We critique each other's pieces and encourage each

other. We talk to each other as writers because that is what we are

striving to be. I remind them that writing is just putting your heart

down on paper. Since we all have a heart that loves things, we all

can put those things down for others to read.

For some children, that means they can use a pen and

paper and scratch all that goodness out. It flows freely and is

amazingly coherent. For others, we use speech-to-text technology

to get their thoughts down on the computer. We don't want them

feeling their brain is working faster than their hands can keep up.

Honestly, if I had to hand write this book, I would still be on the intro. My fingers would be all crippled up and I would be taking Naproxen by the handful.

Their voice is the most important part, not how they get the information down. Stephen Hawking was a world-renowned physicist and cosmologist. His work is not less than because he used technology to get his voice to paper.

At the end of the year, my hope is my children will find their voice. A voice that will help them relate to the world around them. A voice that can honestly, respectfully, and creatively communicate their wants, needs, and desires with those around them. A voice that is a little bit or a lot stronger than when I heard it the first time in August.

The catch is, all the while I am helping others to find their voice, mine often gets quieter. It is as if all the encouraging of others gives me emotional laryngitis. I forget to use my voice. I forget about how important it is for me to stay true to all the things that help my creative juices flow.

All the Things

As mothers it is part of our job to encourage our children to find their voices. Not all of them are going to be poets or authors for National Geographic. However, we encourage them if music is their voice. If they find strength on the stage performing the violin, we take them to the Suzuki lessons and make sure they know how proud we are of their hard work. We tell them practice is important and it will make them stronger.

For those of us who see our athletic children thriving in team sports, we trek thousands of miles for tournaments and shell out enough money to take *really* nice vacations to exotic lands. We wear the team colors and make sure they are all geared up and physically healthy. We see their athletic voice is what makes their heart strongly beat. It is the music that runs through their veins.

Other children show a propensity for art. For them, creativity is something that just emanates from them like breath does for the rest of us. They can make amazing things from clay and watercolor. They see beauty all around and bring that into their art in such a way that we are taken back in wonder and admiration. For those children, we make sure they have art supplies and art classes, as well as enough space to work. We take trips to art museums and point out the beauty of architecture.

All of us want to be heard. All of us want to feel valued for what we feel, believe, and love. Our voice is what opens that door for us. As young children we had things that made us feel heard. Maybe we would draw it with chalk on the sidewalk. Or perhaps we would make it out of sticks in the backyard. Maybe we were heard by the songs we would sing in performances or in our churches. Somewhere along the way however many of us allowed distraction to rob of us of our voices.

Distraction came slowly and stealthily. It is surely a sly one. It came in the needs of mothering you cannot ignore, like the nursing baby who requires your time. It came in the needs of family that must be undertaken. It came in fevers needing to be tended and broken bones requiring surgery. It came in the long hours of working a second job when the bills were piling up.

All the Things

There come times when as a mother we feel lost. We feel we are talking, but nothing of any significant value is coming out. It is not that our loved ones are not listening. It is just that our "voice" has lost its depth. It has forgotten the tune that used to make our heart skip. If you have felt this way, or are feeling this way now, fear not. You can find your voice again. You can find what makes your soul sing.

Think back to what types of childhood hobbies and interests you enjoyed. Did you love to paint or always wanted to? Maybe for you it is going with some other friends and having a night of painting and sisterhood. For others, buying some paper and watercolors at the local craft store and sitting down to paint after the kids go to bed will feed your creative spirit.

Perhaps looking at beautiful photos and putting your stamp on the perspective and focus is your thing. Would taking a photography class get your heart clicking again? Or maybe just taking time to walk through a local botanical garden or park and take some pictures on your own will soothe the shutterbug that has been lonely in your soul.

Many local colleges offer "Furthering Education Classes" that might be the thing you are looking for. Have you always wanted to write and tell your story? Find a writers' group or local conference you could attend. Get a journal and start putting your voice down on paper. Don't worry about it making sense. Just get it out.

Are you funny? Does your heart feel full when you tell stories and make someone laugh? Maybe try your hand at stand-up comedy at a local open mic night. What is the worst that can happen? You get out of the house and unload all the material you have from parenting. It's cheaper than therapy. It's a win win!

Maybe you just need to get back out in nature. See if there are any local hiking groups you could join or get some maps of local hiking trails near your home.

Have you always wanted to learn how to bake beautiful pastries or make sushi from scratch? Many local grocery stores offer cooking classes as well. Grab a group of girlfriends or your hubby and make a date of it.

For those of us with little ones we can't just leave at home, and can't afford babysitting for hours on end, does your local YMCA offer classes you could take a class while using their daycare? Have you always wanted to learn how to play tennis or use weights correctly?

Whatever it is that you do, invest in yourself. Make a commitment to yourself to find your voice. What was once lost can indeed be found again. Tell other moms you are searching for a way to carve out some time to reconnect to things you used to enjoy. Perhaps some of them have ways they can share of how they make that time or what it looks like for them. If they don't already do this for themselves, perhaps you, dedicating time for yourself, will help them to see their worth in terms of needing time of their own. The guilt we feel as moms when we dare take the time for ourselves is such a clever foe.

Most importantly, however, our *children* need to see us

fostering our voice. They need to see us searching and in pursuit. It will show them the importance of keeping it going long after their childhood. Our momma hearts would surely break if after all our efforts to encourage them to use their voice, they became silent once they became adults. So, if we know this to be true, how can we not find our own? We must lead by example. It is truly that simple.

12
OUR VILLAGES

We all have heard the phrase, "It takes a village," which is touted as an African proverb. We can see it on coffee mugs, motivational decor, and the titles of children's books. Ironically, the actual "proverb" has its roots in many societies in Africa. "In Kijita (Wajita) there is a proverb which says 'Omwana ni wa bhone,' meaning regardless of a child's biological parent(s) its upbringing belongs to the community." (Goldberg)

I admit when I was in the pre-parenthood phase of my life, I disagreed wholeheartedly with this phrase. Why would I need other people to help me raise my child? If I couldn't step up and do this on my own, then I had no right to be bringing a child into the world. This young creature was my flesh and my responsibility. Period.

Then I had a baby and all that "I don't need a village" crap went right out the window, along with napping, going to the bathroom in peace, being able to form a complete thought, and fitting back into my pre-preggie pants.

The truth is, across the globe, women help each other in motherhood. We become proverbial villagers and we help each other. From the rice paddies of Thailand to the mountainous regions of Tibet villagers step up. From the Black Hills of South Dakota to the winding Nile villagers offer their expertise. Women are woven together like a maternal tapestry that spans generations and geographic locations. We rely on each other and the support we give each other is essential to effective and healthy parenting. It is also paramount to the overall mental, emotional, and physical health of mothers, young and old.

All the Things

A hobby I have is learning about the cultural similarities of mothering all over the globe. In addition, I find it fascinating how various cultures support new mothers as they find their "parenting legs." From the Netherlands to Nigeria mothers are supported, loved, and treated with the utmost respect after giving birth. From India to Indonesia, mothers and the experience they have had in birthing share many similarities and customs. The one thread that weaves through all the stories is the women are not alone. They have their village and the villagers who have gone before them preparing the map and the way.

In the Netherlands, new mothers receive a personal *"kraamverzorgster"*. This postpartum nurse aids the mother in navigating the new waters of motherhood by offering approximately eight days of personal support in the home of the new mother. The kraamverzorgster keeps track of the health of the baby and mother, but also helps the mother with day-to-day tasks in the home. The nurse may aid in cooking, cleaning, and helping with smaller children who may already be in the home.

All the Things

Since the Netherlands follows a universal health care system, having a kraamverzorgster is not something only the wealthy are able to access. (Mecking)

In similar fashion, new mothers in Japan also have customary support in their home or the home of their families following the birth of a baby. This time after birth has a name all of its own called *"ansei."* It is a peaceful and tranquil time, in which the new mother and baby are pampered by their loved ones. It is encouraged that Japanese mothers stay in bed following the birth of a baby. This allows her body to heal after such an undertaking and offers a quiet time for the bonding of mother and child. In addition, new mothers are fed certain foods that encourage healing of their bodies after childbirth using certain herbs and soups that are easy on the digestive system of both mother and child. (Olsen)

Like in Japan, new mothers in Latin American cultures have their postpartum time called *"La Cuarentena"* which literally translates to "the quarantine." This 40-day time frame is one in

122

which the new mother focuses on healing herself and taking care

of her new baby. New mothers abstain from sexual activity and

household chores. The focus is on integrating the new family unit

and keeping mother and baby away from unhealthy intrusion.

(Olsen)

The list can go on and on in terms of postpartum care.

There are so many similarities and overlapping traditions from

various cultures. Some are connected to Biblical teachings while

others find their roots in Buddhism or Islam. Regardless of the

roots, the fruit being cultivated is a healthy beginning for the new

life that has been created. Across the globe, it is also a time of

recovery for the women who bear this nine-month journey.

My whole childhood I moved from place to place and

made my home amongst the military installations where my

father was stationed. Our village was often transient in nature and

could be packed up in a day or two, only to be moved halfway

across the globe.

All the Things

Most new military mothers I saw didn't have a huge support system that included family close by. If they were lucky, their mothers came and stayed while the new moms convalesced. However, this is not the case for many. Instead, they clung to the other military spouses who understood the temporary nature of their military villages.

These villagers rallied around their military sisters and helped when they could because they knew it soon would be their turn to need help. Some of these relationships would last long after the families relocated to the next duty station, but sometimes they wouldn't. The villagers had helped each other during that harvest or drought season and then they moved on.

Honestly, it wasn't until I became married and moved into our first home that I felt somewhat tethered to one particular location. Even today I get a restless feeling of needing change and I feel the tug of the wanderlust that my early military upbringing planted within me. However, once we were expecting our first child, our village started to appear.

All the Things

It was as if the village was a hazy dreamscape that didn't fully take shape until the need was there. Imagine a Maternal Mary Poppins who blew in when the wind of motherhood began to blow.

While I was expecting our first child, my parents were still devoting their lives to the duty of our country in the Air Force. They came when they could and loved us fiercely, but often they were hundreds of miles away. My village became those who lived in my neighborhood or attended my church. Some were the women I worked with in the school district where I taught. Others I met at the local park when I was waddling my pregnant self in an attempt to not gain the sixty pounds that found their way on my frame.

The women in my life are villagers. The men in my life are villagers too. Some of these villagers play a bigger part in the day-to-day life we lead, and others' roles are small. However, despite the heft of their roles, they all have value in the lives of my children and the health of our family.

All the Things

For some, they were there the minute my children were born. They never wavered in their support, encouragement, and devotion. I would trust these specific villagers with the lives of my children. I know that no matter what, the structure of our inner village is strong and sturdy. These villagers are there for the long haul. They have been, and ever will be, living life with our family every day and in every circumstance. They are villagers bound to us by a bond that transcends all distance and time. Some are villagers by blood, and some are by a sacred bond of *"chosenness."*

Others have come into our village when we needed advice and guidance on topics that lasted days, weeks, or months. They were visitors, if you will, to our village. They brought with them specialized expertise that our small, intimate village was lacking. They brought grace, support, and outside perspective. They brought supplies and techniques that were foreign to us. They stayed for a while and then went on their way, but we celebrate them in our small village and talk about what our lives would be like without their contribution.

I am so thankful for the villager who mentioned to me that I might want to get my son's vision checked. I am also thankful for the villager who diagnosed my then four-year-old son with a "lazy eye." Had it gone undiagnosed much longer, it would have been irreversible. I am ever grateful for that villager's expertise in knowing just which eye exercises were needed. Without their knowledge, my son would have been legally blind in one eye.

How could I, the mother who tucked this small child in at night and kissed his war wounds, miss such a thing? How could I not know that my own child saw two of me? Without these villagers, who knows what the outcome of my son's vision would have been. These villagers had value and purpose.

Some villagers feed us. They feed our souls with words of encouragement and stories of redemption. Others literally feed us. I am ever so grateful for the villager from Ghana who I now call my sister. She lovingly made a traditional rice porridge for me after I suffered from a horrific turn of events after a routine gallbladder removal. Nothing, and I mean nothing was able to be absorbed by my sick body. Her porridge was the only nourishment my body didn't revolt against. She shared the traditional healing method of cooking from her culture and lovingly prepared the food that would aid my healing. She took time from her family to make sure I was able to eat.

Some villagers step right up and into situations when they are not asked. I am ever so grateful for the villager who took my fearful six-year-old son off to the side of his very first hockey game when he was wracked with sobs and paralyzed with fear. This villager saw the need to use humor and focus with my son one on one. He didn't have to do it, but he was part of the bigger picture, saw a need, and stepped in when my son needed the support of someone other than his mom. He was a part of our village and filled a need that day. He encouraged toughness through timidity. We have not seen him since that season ended, but his impact left a positive stamp on the heart of my boy.

All the Things

In am forever indebted to the villager who took my daughter, at age five months, when my cherub could barely sit up, and nurtured her while I was working. Ironically, before she was my villager, I was hers.

I taught two of her three daughters as their 8th grade Language Arts teacher. With her taking in my girl, our village fabric became more intricate and the weave became tighter. She knew how my momma heart was heavy with the guilt of returning to work and being away from my baby girl. I shared with her how I had longed to stay home with the birth of each of my children. For nearly four years, day in and day out, this villager loved my girl as her own flesh and blood. She is forever bound to our village and has a special place in our hearts.

Our pediatrician, our dentist, our pastor, our neighbors, our church family, and teachers all form the outlying village my children live in. They interact with these villagers and although they don't sit at our dinner table with us each night, it doesn't mean their involvement in my children's lives is any less important. They are just needed in different capacities and span different timeframes.

I think back to my pre-parenthood way of thinking and laugh at how high and mighty I thought I was. It was really delusional thinking, if we are being transparent, to think that I could do the hardest job on the planet all by myself. Really? Where did I get the idea that doing this job by myself would somehow garner me a special "I Did it Myself New Mom" award? I'll tell you where we get it from. We get it from the media who are always telling us to do more, be more, achieve more. We were never meant to do ALL THE THINGS.

However, so many of us try. We give it the old college try! We head to Target long before the *"La Cuarentena"* is over. Heck, we are walking around our neighborhood or signing up for postpartum yoga on day 7!

Sweet sisters, I challenge you to just take a minute. Take a lesson from our Japanese sisters and just rest. Don't feel that you need to do it all on your own. Look for your village. It is there. It will look different for all of us, but it is there. Don't shy away from asking those villagers to step foot in your messy, untidy, exhausted house. Let those villagers serve you with their gifts. By not letting them in, you are denying them their expertise and craft.

And sisters who have already gone down the path a time or too, look for where your talents and gifts can be used for the betterment of new moms. For when we live in a village, we are stronger. Like a physical village, we are closer. We are there to huddle together and form a windbreak against the storms of life. When the bitterness of winter seasons catches us frozen in fear, we offer and are offered warmth and support. We dig the trenches and make firebreaks when the heat of summer seasons bears down and wildfires erupt. We offer guidance and experience. I would much rather navigate what comes my way with others standing by my side. I am a villager through and through.

13
A Balanced Climb

New beginnings are an exciting time. Things are both fresh and fragile. There is both an anticipation and wonder of what will be. It is a time of learning and exploration as well as reflection and planning.

New beginnings are also just that-- new. They give us a chance to start over with a fresh slate. Maybe it is a new haircut, a new house, a new job, or even just a new daily routine. The amazing part of this is that each day we are greeted with newness, even if we don't change anything about our lives. The fact that the day starts over fresh and new is our reset button. We even can hit

that reset button in the middle of the day. It is our choice.

Yet many of us, myself included, rush through our

routines with to-do lists that never get completed and end our

days with just as much frustration and stress as the day before.

Friends, we need to stop this cycle.

It is draining our joy and the ability for us to focus on the

newness all around us. It affects our health, our relationships, and

all that makes us gifts to the world. It also robs us of being present

to see the giftedness in others we love and hold dear.

Recently, I almost missed the sprouting of seedlings

planted in the hopes of future summer blooms. I had made the

environment all warm and healthy for them. I gave them a great

area by the window with just enough sun and moisture in their

dome. I followed all the directions on how to take good care to

place them in the perfect position for growth. I was diligent. There

they were, pushing up through their nutrient rich soil. However,

because I was so distracted by life, I almost missed it.

All the Things

That specific day had been filled with driving in pouring rain back and forth across the Mississippi River hither and yon. By the time I came home my head was splitting, my mind was numb, and the coffee I thought would be a magical elixir had failed. I needed to hit the reset button.

For me, that meant I needed a nap.

I needed to stop.

I needed to rest.

So, I did.

Here's the thing. So many times, we just keep going. We continue to push through because that little voice in our head tells us this is what society says we should do. We should be able to spin 7,893 plates all at once because we are strong, smart, wise, wonder women. And don't get me wrong, because truly you are all of the above.

You are strong.

You are smart.

You are wise.

All the Things

And yes, many small people in our lives consider us superheroes in our own right because of the magic lassos we wield so effortlessly.

However, we must remember that to keep our strength up we need to rest. We need to feed ourselves both nutritionally and soulfully. We need to drink in the words of other friends who can fill our cups when we draw near to the bottom. And sometimes we need to ask for a refill, again and again.

Many of us thirst for support, yet we sit dehydrated in darkness because we fear being judged. Asking for support is not a sign of weakness. It is a sign you are nourishing yourself from the inside out and you're smart enough to know you can't do it alone.

And you have the market cornered on smarts. You know when you are wavering. You know when you are carrying too much. Honestly, come on. We know that *no one* can balance and spin 7,893 plates. It is impossible. Yet we continue to try. Who really lives in those Pinterest houses after all?

All the Things

Unfortunately, the reality is the more we add to our balancing act, the more certain plates fall. They break and are not replaced. This is fine for hobbies that once filled our time like scrapbooking and knitting. Those plates don't have hearts.

But sometimes our spinning causes plates with hearts and eyes to lose their balance as well. These plates are relationships that fall to the ground, crack, and roll far out of our reach. We say we will pick them up another time, but we don't. These plates are not easily glued back together.

There are plates of our children, who we know are not replaceable, yet we continue to spin them and sometimes at a fast speed. Their view of the world is being shaped by what they see us doing. Their view of their place in that world is directly proportional to how we plant and position them.

We sign them up for more and more activities thinking it will fill their cups and possibly give them an advantage. We race from one event to another not really enjoying where we are or being excited about where we are going. We are checking off the boxes. Our children register this. It becomes programmed in their brains as how adulting works. They will think this is normal. We know this is not normal because we remember when it wasn't so.

We remember a time when kids were able to be kids. We remember a time when our mothers sent us outside and told us to come back in when the lights were coming on. Kids didn't have daily standing playdates or crazy sports calendars. More doesn't make our children better.

It makes them stressed.

It makes us stressed.

And they will grow to think this stress is the normal donning of the clothes of adulthood. We are layering them up early for the long-term weather forecast. When really, sister, all they need are people in their lives who support them emotionally, nurture them spiritually, give them enough sunshine, and make sure they are hydrated properly. We have them layered up for the next ice age when we know most kids want to play in the snow without a jacket on for goodness sakes.

All the Things

We are *wiser* than this. We read blogs, we watch videos, we share things with each other, and we know this wisdom brings awareness. We know time is finite and we only have so much of it. Yet we continue to be drawn into doing more, being more, and having more. Instead we need to focus on doing less, being content, and having enough.

Balance is the key to success in so many things. Without it, music would have an irritating ding to it, rather than a smooth melody. A bike rider would never experience the thrill of air in their face without it. An unbalanced room seems drafty or cold, while one that has just the right composition is inviting, cozy, and feels pulled together. A balanced budget allows for the needs and wants of a household within its means. But all too often as mothers we are far from balanced.

As a mother I struggle with taking time for myself even when it is a small nap or simply putting my feet up with a cup of tea. I have a plethora of excuses that come so quickly into my head as to why I can't do something for myself. Usually it is because my children need to do this, or they must go there. When really, a lot of the time the fact is I am either too tired to focus on myself or I think others will think it selfish for me to take time and just be gone from the parenting parade.

But the crux of the issue is, that when we *don't* take the time, the balance is so off kilter that we aren't able to do anything well. Everything we do is off and can look a lot like a rider on a bike with a wobbly wheel, or sound like a ballad without a chorus. We are plugging away, but we are *not* pulled together. We don't think clearly or parent with patience because our gas tank is empty, and our tires are out of alignment.

Sometimes we all need to get away. We need to leave everything behind and take a breath, or two, or three. We need to readjust our perspective on those *things* which are important. This is not easy in the lives we lead. The lives filled with demands, responsibilities, and expectations.

We need to give ourselves the gift of time. Time away from all that usually makes it hard for us to think. We need to refuel our tanks and take time to process. We all need to breathe deeply and work on finding clarity.

Recently I needed to step away. A simple nap was not going to suffice. I needed space. I needed quiet. I did this to recharge my batteries and get my wheels aligned.

I longed to hike without having to listen to children complain about how hot they were, or how tired they were, or asking how much longer it was.

I wanted to go kayaking and not have to worry about keeping a visual on my three lovebugs and wondering if their life jackets were truly going to protect them or if it was time to reapply sunscreen.

I needed to be able to just lie in bed and contemplate if I wanted to get up that day, versus being pulled out of bed with questions regarding the morning menu or a needed hand in the bathroom. I yearned to be able to have adult conversations with my sister friends about adult issues and not have to worry about young ears who may be scarred by such talk. My soul needed this time.

For me, I feel most recharged when I have visited with old friends. Friends who knew me long before I was a mother. Friends who I have no reason to try to impress. Friends who remember when life was far less complicated and demanding. Friends who listen and share in the same struggles of motherhood.

It is a fold that I belong to. A fabric of who I am to have these friendships that have stood the test of time and distance. It is a true treasure to be able to pick up right where we left off the last time we were able to take a breath and connect.

During these times together we have talked, we have cried. We have shared in great wine and played roulette for the first time. We usually get way too little sleep and see beautiful sights.

These friends are those who don't care about the physical me. They care about the emotional, mental, and spiritual me. Whether or not I have used dry shampoo for a couple of days is inconsequential. These are the friends who I can be real with and raw with.

In the safety of their fold, I can not only share but dissect and investigate my fears and failures. I dump out all the feelings of inadequacy and share the dreams I dare to bring to the light of day.

It is not just a "me fest" mind you. We all have our time, and it allows us to have a type of purse cleanout, but for our hearts. You know what that looks like and when it's needed ladies. There is so much junk in there creating havoc in our hearts.

There are receipts of things we bought into and planned on returning but never did. There are things we said we would just keep a little longer because we might find the thing that would make it just right. But in the end, we realize there is nothing in our mortal power to make that thing whole. It is just taking up prime real estate in our hearts. It creates distress for us to have to navigate through all the "stuff" in our hearts that is simply a distraction from what is the most important parts of our sweet lives.

When we clean out our real purses, they are literally lighter. They are easier to carry. It is amazing how much lighter my purse is when I gather up all that change and invest it in something more purposeful than rolling around in the dark recesses of my purses' pockets.

It is the same when we clean out our hearts from the excess and superfluous. Taking stock of what we are carrying and why allows us to clear things out. Our journey from there on does tend to feel lighter. It makes moving forward and going to new places a lot easier. We can move forward without the heaviness of being held back by that which was never there to be helpful on our journey in the first place.

Many times, when I am with my chosen sisters, we go out in nature. We hike, we talk, or we just quietly move together toward a common goal in silence. This is where I feel my withered soul being slowly nursed back to hydration.

All the Things

One day, we were hiking in the Desolate Wilderness of Tahoe in Northern California. We were headed to Eagle Lake and toward one of the most beautiful and peaceful spots I have ever seen.

However, I almost couldn't focus on all the beauty around me. It was a tough hike. Well, for me, it was a tough one. I was struggling with the altitude and sucking wind. I had told myself I would be more in shape for this trip, but remember that "not taking time for myself" issue? Well, yeah. Suffice to say, procrastination was not my friend on this hike.

The issue wasn't even that I was slow. Each step, if not taken correctly, could lead to quite an injury on unforgiving rocks. So, my eyes were constantly down. My mind was looking for just the right foothold. And sometimes, okay, more than a couple times I had to stop. I had to catch my breath.

I was hoping some kind and thoughtful eagle scout had put a "little free library" up here in the wilderness with perhaps some "little free oxygen tanks" for those of us out of shape mommas. No luck.

But stopping was a gift. Stopping forced me to look around. It wasn't until I was forced to stop that I saw all the beauty around me, all the natural wonders that are gifts to us. The tall trees and bright green moss. The flowing water coming from snowcapped mountains.

And when I stopped, and when I adjusted my focus to what was surrounding me, I was able to catch my breath. I was able to take a moment and get the energy to keep climbing.

My friend, who has hiked this path many times before me, just waited patiently. She didn't rush me. She didn't tease me for having to breathe. She too just looked around and saw the beauty.

The view once we made it to Eagle Lake was so worth the climb. While I was on this trek up the mountain it hit me, how hard it is to *really* see what is happening around you.

All the Things

Looking at life, the climb is often rough. We are focusing on the here and now, the mundane and rote. We are so worried about the next step and not falling flat on our faces either literally or metaphorically. The beauty and relationships that surround us are lost while we trudge a path that often sucks the wind right out of us. Often, we are so distracted we aren't seeing the "seedlings" we so lovingly guide, actually push up through the difficulties surrounding them.

Life is hard. There is often no official trail guide telling us what step to take and which rock to avoid. Our footholds must be our own. It makes the journey ours. But sometimes in life, there are friends who have been where you have been. They have navigated those trails. They have tripped. They have fallen. They have the scars to prove it. They have also seen the beauty around the next bend, but they don't hurry you through the trails. They just wait for you a couple of paces ahead, quietly encouraging, and giving the gift of patience, because they know your strength. They know you will get there, and once you do, what a beautiful sight there is to behold.

These are my lifelines; my soul hydration stations. My chosen sisters who fill me up so I can in turn fill up my people. It is a cyclical love affair of the heart. We love others so they can love. We encourage others so they can encourage. They are gifts from my Heavenly Father sent down to remind me of how loved I am by Him.

It is funny to me that I have a sticker on my van window that reminds me of when I need to change the oil in my van. Going too long over that number means the engine is going to get gunky and not work properly. I wouldn't want my van, the vehicle I rely on daily, to fail. So, I make sure I get it checked out regularly. Yet too often I don't treat as tenderly the vehicle that has gotten me this far in life, my own human body.

For within myself I carry other precious things. I carry a hope for the future, strength for the test, and patience for the next bend in the road. I carry endurance for the hike, a vision for what can be, and the perseverance of finding passion in life. However, the tasks of motherhood often pile on top of these other precious things. We all need to step away. We need to regroup, reframe, and recharge.

This was precious time I deserved. I am worth that and so are you sweet sister. We all are. Find what makes you balanced and commit to allowing yourself that time.

God tells us the importance of friends who support and encourage us. He reminds us of the need for community as we face both the trials and the celebrations of life.

In Proverbs 17:17 he says, "A friend loves at all times." This means our true friends, despite their personal views on choices we have made or whether they agree with our current path, love us. Their support flows unconditionally and without judgment. They may share wisdom with us, but true friends don't judge.

In Proverbs 27:17 He says, "Iron is made sharp with iron, and one man is made sharp by a friend." We are literally stronger together with other women who lift us up. We are each other's iron support beams. We are riveted together with experiences and trials only women understand.

And my personal favorite, in Proverbs 27:9 he reminds us that when we are feeling rundown and dehydrated by life's constant demands, "The heartfelt counsel of a friend is as sweet as perfume and incense." Who are the soul refreshers in your life? Who are your people when you are needing a lift? Who makes your life sweet with their presence? Can you picture their smiles? Can you hear their laughs? What is your history and how did your paths cross?

How can you make some time to reconnect or find your

people? This time will look different for each momma. It must. We all balance things differently.

Our lives are so tightly bound and simultaneously fraying. It is a beautiful fabric with so many complexities and interwoven idiosyncrasies. Because our needs for recharge are so vast, for some a night at a local coffee house fills their cup. Some sisters feel full after a day away, while for others a weekend suffices.

For me, that year, that summer, it was a week in the golden hills of northern California with friends who have known me since I was a girl. With friends who know my struggles and strengths, as well as I know theirs.

It was a summer I was reminded that the climb is not the important part of life. It is the ability to truly take in the beauty we walk in every step along the way. It was a reminder to stop and truly see the new beauty in "seedlings" pushing through. It reminded me to lift my eyes and see the beauty that surrounds us in the friendships and relationships that help us along the way.

All the Things

And when you tire, because we all do, sometimes all we need is a

good friend, just standing next to us in silence as we catch our

breath. True friends, however, would pack an extra oxygen tank.

14
$151.20

After I was well along expecting our third child, my
fingers were a little less svelte than they were on our wedding
day. Okay, in all honesty, they were much like the shape of
canned sausages and it wasn't just my fingers. We decided to be
honest with each other a couple of chapters ago. Remember we
are working on not judging.

The beautiful wedding set my husband had lovingly
picked out for me was not even able to squeeze on my pinky
finger. Therefore, I took to wearing a plain silver band my
husband had gotten at some local pawn shop.

All the Things

It worked for what I needed and then after my daughter was born, I upgraded to have three thin rings with my children's names etched on them. I would rotate wearing one each day, because surprisingly even after a couple of months, my svelte fingers didn't return as quickly as they had left.

I didn't really care, and I continued wearing those rings on and off for the next nine years. Sometimes, if the stars aligned, I was dehydrated, and perhaps the temperature was nearing the freezing mark, I might be able to squeeze on just my wedding band, but most days, nothing fell into place that easily.

In many ways, I felt my life was not in alignment either. I had left a job I felt called to leave, only to have the job I thought was a "Godsend" fall through two short years later. I had taken a 50% pay cut leaving the first job. Then I took a 100% pay cut when the second one ended.

Since I was 16 years old, I had always worked in some shape or fashion. Before being married I supported myself and lived on my own. In my married life I had always brought in "my share" to the household. To think I was bringing in nothing was terrifying.

I was also the household "budget girl." I knew the numbers and without overtime it was going to be *tight*. How was this going to work? Was this a smart move? Was I listening to God calling me to be home or was I being irresponsible?

I was trying very hard to feel God had me right where I needed to be, but sometimes I can be a little controlling and want to put myself where I think I need to be. Up until this time I really couldn't tell if my decisions were being made to fulfill my own personal desires or if it was truly God's will for me to be home and focus on my family.

Then early this summer, my daughter was helping me clean the top of my dresser and opened my jewelry drawer. She was in awe of the set of rings that were sitting there just waiting for their turn to see the light again.

"Mom, what are these? Are these your wedding rings?" she asked.

"Yes, Sis, they are."

"Um, why aren't you wearing them? They're

BEAUTIFUL!!!!!"

"I actually can't quite fit them on my fingers now. My

fingers are a little wider than they used to be when Daddy first

gave them to me."

"Well, that is easy to fix. We just need to have them sized.

We should take them to the jewelry store. They can do that for

you. Did you know that, Mom?"

Her sweet innocence and helpful heart were beautiful.

Obviously, I knew they could. But in all honesty, I didn't really

have the money in the budget. It was always one thing or another

and I knew getting two rings sized wasn't going to be an easy

twenty bucks. So, I had just accepted the fact that maybe one day,

I would have them back on my finger.

There were also many times in those nine years that our

marriage was less than stellar. There were times I didn't care that I

couldn't put those rings back on my finger. I was mad. I was angry. I threw pity parties. This marriage thing was **hard,** and I didn't *like* it. Why couldn't things be easy like other people's lives seemed. Why did it always seem we were two steps behind?

So, there I was, with my sweet daughter telling me she had it all figured out, and there I was wondering if this was how God was speaking to me. Through the loving simple words of my daughter.

I decided to go to the jewelers and at least get the rings cleaned. I would ask them how much it would cost and maybe I could have it be a birthday or Christmas present. Maybe I could save some money here and there to put toward the cost. I honestly had no idea how much it was going to cost to get the job done.

So, I reached down into the drawer and took out the original box my husband gave me the day he proposed. I put them gently back in the box for traveling. However, before I could close the drawer a small bag caught my eye.

I had forgotten I had taken a couple gold earrings that were missing their mates, broken necklace pieces, and some gold beads that were tarnished and dented and put them in that bag. I had thought about having them melted down at one time, or thought about trading them in, but hadn't gotten to it. I had completely forgotten that small bag was even there tucked far from my daily view.

So, I thought, what the heck. Maybe this will add up to a couple bucks and take some money off the total.

My daughter and I headed out to the jewelers which was across town. Once we were there, I asked the jeweler to simply clean the piece and give me an amount for how much the sizing would be. I mentioned to her that I didn't have the money to do it now, but just wanted to know for budgeting purposes. She was kind and sized my finger for both rings.

They each needed to go up 1.5 sizes. She went over to the calculator and looked up current gold prices. She came back and told me the total for both rings would be $151. 10. I thanked her and then remembered my small clear bag of mismatched, broken, and dented gold.

All the Things

"Could you please tell me if this is worth anything? I am not even sure if it is all real gold, honestly. I thought maybe it might take a little bit off my total," I inquired.

"Absolutely. Let me go and check it out in the back with one of my jewelers and weigh it," she responded.

She went to the back and I continued looking at the other lovely pieces in the various jewelry counters. The lights shone down on various gems and they dazzled with brilliance. I ran into a friend who was looking for a graduation gift and we began to chit chat and catch up. She asked me how I was doing, and how I liked being home and not working full-time.

Honestly, I can say that question was a loaded one. Each time someone asked me, I was not sure how to answer. Part of me felt like telling them I was great and felt like being home was exactly where I was supposed to be.

Other times I felt like I was wrestling with "imposter syndrome." I said everything was good, but was I really doing what I was supposed to be doing? Imposter syndrome is when you feel everyone else sees you doing a good job at whatever your job may be. However, on the inside, you feel so shallow. The truth is that everything is hanging in a delicate balance that seems so fragile. The "good job" everyone else sees is just barely paper thin, and if they looked too closely, perhaps what they would really see is all a sham.

I honestly told her the first year was a big learning curve for all of us and being home had given me a sense of time and less rushing around than I had ever had in my adult life. I honestly told her it seemed weird not going all the time but is also nice to let our normal body rhythms tell us when to get up, and when to go to sleep.

I continued that it was nice to not have to worry about covering for lesson plans if my kids are sick and need to stay home. And don't get me started on the fact that the "laundry dragon" had finally been partially slayed. We both laughed, and she agreed that particular dragon is a big one she had yet to conquer.

All the Things

At that time, the cashier called my name and was ready to check me out. She then asked me with a quizzical look in her eyes, "Are you ready?"

"Yeah, I am good," I replied.

"No, are you *really* ready?" she asked again.

"I guess so. I mean, I thought I was ready. Is there something wrong?" I asked.

"I have worked here for longer than I can remember. This is my family's store. I have **never** had this happen before," she said.

At this point, I was completely confused, and I am sure the look on my face displayed this concern. She continued, "The gold you brought in is worth $151.20."

"Wait, what?" I asked.

"Yes. Your total for the sizing is $151.10 and the total for your gold is $151.20."

"So basically, you are telling me that you owe me ten cents back?" I questioned.

All the Things

"Yeah, that is what I am telling you. I have no idea how this is possible. It is just crazy. In all my years of working here, I have never had something like this happen. I have been here for over 20 years," she continued.

I stood there and just smiled. I knew exactly why it was happening and who was responsible for it. I knew who had orchestrated it all and who was trying to talk to me. My loving God was sending me a modern-day burning bush in the form of a ring that had long needed to be returned to my finger.

I explained to her, "I know exactly how this is happening. A year ago, I took a leap of faith to leave my full-time job and come home. I decided to focus on homeschooling my children and was very worried about how it would work out. How would we be able to afford things that come up, just like this? This is how God is reminding me that he has me covered, and then some."

She stood there astounded. She listened with a huge smile on her face. After I was done, she said, "That is the coolest story I have ever heard. Thank you so much for sharing that with me. I can't wait to go home and tell my husband. So Cool!"

I could have just kept the backstory to myself, said thank you, and left the shop that day. But here's the deal, the story of how God is showing up in our lives daily needs to be shared.

People are hurting.

People are scared.

People are worried about how they are going to keep going. They all need to hear how God is ever present in our lives. He has us in the palm of his hand and is there for us "and then some." He is ever present in our lives each day. Now when I look down at my shiny pair of rings, I am reminded daily of his faithfulness. I don't need these metal bands to truly know he loves me beyond measure, but it was a great way to be reminded. He knew his child was doubting, so he sent me a message to say, *"Hey! I got you! Stop worrying and just listen."*

All the Things

In 2 Corinthians 9:8 NLT it says, "And God will generously provide all you need. Then you will always have everything you need, and plenty left over to share with others."

When you look closely at what you need, how is God showing you he is faithful? How is he providing for you and those you love?

In what ways is he trying to communicate with you? He is the author of our love languages. How is he trying to get your attention?

Is it in the smile from the person in the grocery line? Is it in the text you get from a long-lost friend at just the right time? Is it in a refund you get from something you overpaid, and it pays a new bill you weren't expecting? Is it in the form of a beautiful sunset at the close of a hectic or horrible day?

And most importantly, when these messages happen? How are you sharing them with others?

15
GRATITUDE PIE

Fall is one of my favorite seasons. In the Midwest fall is a tad elusive. It might not show its cooler hand until mid to late September. Sometimes the temperature feels more like summer until the first couple weeks of October. Despite these warm days, festivals and fall favorites abound. From corn mazes and apple picking farms to pumpkin patches, one can find something for the family to have fun doing. Over the years, we have made it a tradition to go apple picking.

For all practical purposes we can easily get a bag of apples from the local grocery store for less than five dollars compared to spending five, six, or eight times that amount at a local apple farm.

However, that is not the point. The point is making memories and those are not made by picking up a bag of apples at Aldi. The memories are seared into our hearts by getting out into nature and taking in all that is apple picking.

It starts with sunny skies. My favorite type of day to go apple picking must have sunny skies. It has the type of crisp blue sky that offers that backdrop against the sea of green leaves and parallel rows of trees laden with fruit with nary a cloud to count. Some years we have sweat while picking. Other years we were bundled up and our noses were red with the crisp fall breeze.

But the sun, oh the sun makes the memories that much more brilliant. My heart carries these memories safely from the very first year of my kids toddling the rows to pick their first apple to the angsty teen years when they quietly sit the entire way in the minivan with earbuds pushing out the familial world.

All the Things

Once we arrive with bags in hand the true hunt ensues. They begin scoping out of what trees have the fruit that beckons to be picked. From toddling to standing on tippy toes, to towering over many of the branches they search for the perfect round, delicious fruit. Sometimes they do this together and work a single tree while peering in and showing each other where the best apple is. Other times they venture off on their own to scout out their own juicy, crisp, perfectly sphere-shaped bounty.

They quickly find picking the perfect apple is no easy task. Some are not yet ripe and stay firmly held in place despite their eager tugs. Others have already been plagued by insects who beat their young hands to the fragrant fruit. Others have become split or mushy. Some, although they look so inviting, are just out of reach and will stay put. Others look perfect but must be grabbed through branches and leaves that brush my children's faces and force them to create new game plans.

As my children work their way through the trees with bags that quickly become heavier and heavier, I follow behind them taking it all in. They diligently try to both help each other and at the same time playfully out pick each other when it comes to finding perfection amongst the rows.

Once our bags are full, we head to check out and make our way home. Our senses, our hearts, and our tummies are usually all filled up and we are ready to come home and make something yummy with our pick of the day. If we are lucky, we might even get some equally delicious apple cider and cinnamon doughnuts to go with our treasured apples.

This year was no different and once home my son decided to find a recipe for apple pie. I had a family favorite of my mom's apple pie, so we decided on that. We washed our apples and got all our ingredients out. In that moment, it hit me as to how much work goes into the making of an apple pie.

For years, when I was younger, I would sit and watch my mom make apple pies. Truth be told, many years I didn't want to watch. In my angsty teen years I am sure I would rather have done anything else. However, as an adult and a mom now I am grateful she took the time to have me watch, observe, and take it all in.

Once I was old enough to help, I learned the way she peeled her apples and the perfect thickness the slices needed to be so the pie filling wouldn't be too mushy after baking. I was told the secrets about thickening with flour for the perfect filling and the ice-cold water needed for the flakiest of crusts.

Now that I am a mom, I do the same with my kiddos. But as I sat there with them in eager anticipation of their first attempt and lesson on making an apple pie, something hit me about our preparation. We were only one small part of this apple pie that would in a few hours be in our bellies. They would joyfully say, "Look what I made!" upon the completion of such an undertaking. However, they were not alone in that process. They were simply finishing and fine tuning the work so many other people had done up to that point.

I remembered something a dear friend once told me about gratitude. When she used to be caught driving over the

All the Things

Mississippi River from St. Louis, Missouri to her small farm back in Illinois she would often find herself in rush hour traffic. I asked her if it bothered her to have to make that drive every day. She said she would try to not get distracted by the time it was taking to get from work to home. She would look at all that went into the journey.

She shared that instead of being irritated by being behind the stinky trash truck, she would be grateful for the worker who picked up the refuse, so our streets were clean. Instead of being bothered by the truckers who were on either side of her, she was grateful for the drivers who were hauling food, fuel, or building materials so others would have what they needed for their jobs. She was grateful for them taking time away from their families to do their job and do it safely.

Her words then made me start thinking of things differently in terms of the things that I use in my home daily. But the day we were making our apple pie my thoughts shifted to all those who had done work earlier than the day we simply picked the apples that were ready.

What went on to get us to this point? How was a mist-laden jungle in Sri Lanka or a water buffalo connected to our apple pie today?

You see, just when we think we are doing something as simple as making an apple pie on a crisp Midwest fall day, we find ourselves connected with people, animals, and the world as a community. We are in our kitchens washing and peeling apples we picked in an orchard in Southern Illinois with our own hands. But what about the other hands that got us to this point? Where are? Who are they? What are their lives like?

First, we can start in our own town in the orchard that our hands touched. Did you know it takes roughly five to eight years before the average apple tree is ready to bear fruit? That means the orchard owner in our town tended to, cared for, and nurtured those trees for almost the age of my nine-year-old daughter. That orchard owner pruned those trees annually in every year of her life before her hands even picked that first apple. He was

preparing those trees to produce the finest fruit for future apple

lovers.

Remember that mist laden jungle? How is that connected

to our American apple pie baking in my oven? Have you ever

been to Sri Lanka? What about Myanmar or Sumatra? Ever sat on

a cart behind a water buffalo? Well you might not have but the

cinnamon sitting in your kitchen cabinet sure has.

Your ground cinnamon started off as a tree growing for at

least three years in the jungle of these countries before its bark and

small limbs were harvested for this brown aromatic spice. It is

hand harvested by skilled craftsman who take the bark right off

the trees and painstakingly make sure it remains in one piece

while they roll it up and take it out of the jungle on flat sleds

pulled by water buffaloes.

They then dry the bark for at least a week turning the bark,

or quills, over to ensure proper and even drying. These then

become the coiled quills we buy in packages at grocery stores or ground up in containers to easily measure out for our pies. There

is nothing easy about this type of work for the villager traipsing

with machetes through the jungles to get this special spice.

We can look at all the things we needed to make that

simple apple pie. We could ask questions like *Where did the tree*

come from that our cutting board and rolling pin were made from? How

much wheat would we need to make two cups of flour? What is the name

of the farmer and where are the fields where our flour was grown? Who

forged the sharpened knife that allowed me to slice my apples so quickly?

The questions could go on and on.

I can go on Amazon and quickly order all the supplies

needed to make an apple pie in one click. It will be delivered to

our door in 24 hours. With this ability to access "things" it makes

it too easy for our children to miss the work that goes into getting

these things from their beginning to our consumption. It becomes

too easy for them to become self-centered and believe they are

self-reliant.

All the Things

Our ability to connect so quickly through technology often takes away the actual art of *real* connectivity.

It isn't until we stop.

It isn't until we think.

It isn't until we see our world as the interconnected web of life that it is.

To do that we must ask the questions like children do when their minds are free of distractions. They ask the "hows and whys" and want to know where things come from. They do this to make sense and connect things to themselves. As parents we all know this time in parenting a toddler is exhausting.

However, somewhere along the way, both children and adults stop asking those questions and just start accepting that things are automatically there, present, and ready for us to have. It is only when we stop and adjust our perspective that we truly see the magnificent connections we have with all living and breathing people and animals throughout the world.

All the Things

Children need to be taught to think about this connection because it is how we understand our place in the world. It reminds us that our place is no different than others, and we rely on others we will never meet for many of our needs to be met.

What about that cinnamon harvester? Does he realize his life's work touches the lives of so many people all over the world? Does he know the bark he scrapes off those trees is added to tea in India that warms hearts and bellies in cups of chai tea measured by the ton?

Does he know his spice travels over 5,000 miles to the home of the Eiffel Tower and finds itself wrapped lovingly by the hands of French pastry chefs as they create mouthwatering cinnamon rolls?

Would he do his job any differently knowing his hands help nourish the mouths and bodies of people throughout the world? That shelves throughout North America and Europe are lined with jars of his handiwork ready for shoppers to take home and make an apple pie with?

All the Things

Just like our pie, our lives are often far more complex than we even know. Our experiences and spiritual gifts have the power to transcend time, distance, and geographical boundaries.

We have ingredients that have been gathered far and wide in our lives. We have had people tend our branches and feed our souls.

We have had people who toiled for years making sure our tender hearts were protected from things that would harm the precious fruits of our spirits. They have worked with their hands with precision and care to help us navigate the peeling of our layers to get to the sweet spices of life.

These craftsmen walked through the jungles and orchards of our lives in the forms of parents, teachers, pastors, coaches, doctors, and friends. They were divinely placed to help prune, support, and nurture.

These craftsmen stood side by side with us and sweated in the heat of the summers of our lives. They made sure in the torrential rains of spring that we didn't wash away or lose our roots. They weathered the winters when our brittle branches were bare to the brutal winds and they prayed we would survive. They rejoiced when the warmth would return to our lives and our true harvest would begin.

Many of us have had people praying for us long before we were even born or thought of. Many of us have had friends of friends who have added our names or needs to their prayers without us ever even meeting them.

You see, too often we think we have arrived somewhere all on our own. We celebrate our accomplishments and all the hard work we put in. We think we have made our own pie. We stand tall beaming at what *we* have done. This is simply faulty and dangerous ground to tread. This concept leads to grandiose thinking. It breeds feelings and thoughts that we are superior or have such unique qualities that are unmatched by others. Maintaining this perspective of our lives will lead to a distorted view of reality.

All the Things

To counter this we need to add more gratitude. We need to add it lavishly in all things we do. We need to dump it by the truckload anywhere we can.

We need to foster this ingredient in the hearts of our children. We need it to be a "nurtured wired" question like *How does it get here? Who works hard to create it?* We know it is not a "hard wired" one in this world of fast paced self-gratification.

As parents we are entrusted with tending to, nurturing, and God willing seeing the harvest in our children's lives. However, just like the cinnamon harvester we don't always know how far and wide the "spice" in our children's lives will go. We can't always see how their spice will mingle with others and make beautiful things that will bless our world.

But we do know that God knows. He promises us that. He tells us in Jeremiah 29:11, "For I know the plans I have for you," declares the Lord, "plans to prosper you and not to harm you, plans to give you hope and a future."

I am that "you."

All the Things

You are that "you."

Our children are that "you."

A farmer in Minnesota is that "you."

A cinnamon harvester in Myanmar is that "you."

It is only together we make a recipe. Individually we are only parts of God's amazing cookbook.

I want my children, when they serve that apple pie as adults, not to say "Look what **I** made" but rather, "Look what I had a part in." I want them to think of life as a huge "gratitude pie."

I want them to understand they are a piece to the intricate and beautiful part of our world's story.

Of God's story.

And more importantly I want them to see the importance and value of others.

Yes, I know that without them my life wouldn't be nearly as sweet, but without others too, life would be bland. We need

All the Things

that complexity and flavor from all that makes this world

beautiful, intricate, and divinely connected.

We need that spice in life and sometimes that spice might

just come bundled lovingly in quills from the jungles of Sri Lanka

being pulled by a water buffalo.

16
GUARD RAILS

An area of parenthood never really addressed much in the early years is one that has taken me by surprise. The mere mention of the words makes seasoned parents cringe or shake their heads. They may even make a sign of the cross over you or offer to meet you for drinks later in the week. When you enter this stage of parenting, you are literally sitting in the passenger seat of death *every time*.

This stage has two simple words. Two words that have the power to turn up anxiety levels of the most seasoned of parents.

NEW DRIVER

All the Things

The irony is that as a teen I remember being so ready for the freedom driving would bring. I was excited to be visiting my friends and getting my first job, meeting for after school functions and just feeling like I had nothing holding me down. Well, maybe the speed limit, but you get the point. For teens, this time is so exciting!!!

For parents, this time is everything *but* exciting.

I am a confessed control freak. I understand this. My husband knows this. It has taken me quite a while to fully accept this and find ways to not let this affect and impact the spontaneous joy that is parenting and living life to the fullest.

Let me be perfectly transparent here. There is *no joy* in sitting in the passenger seat, while you are slowly starting to straddle that white line on the right side of the road. Spontaneity is not your friend when a new driver decides to tap the brake a little too strong.

Do you remember those "others" who I thought liked to add drama to life? I am *not* being one of them right here. I am completely being truthful. You will think you are drifting to the edge of death as your driver hugs that right line. You will wish you had superpowers to push that wheel with the power of your mind.

In all honesty, what is happening in real time is that your life is quite frankly flashing in front of your eyes.

Did I make sure the will is up to date?

Have I made my final wishes very clear to my loved ones?

Did I sign my donor card the last go around?

Am I wearing clean underwear?

You get the idea.

Having a new driver is the epitome of going "cold turkey" for us control freaks. We can't have it both ways. I can't scream because then I know there will be a crash. I can't take over, because the whole idea is to teach teens how to handle themselves and these exact situations. I can't have him stay in a booster seat, drinking out of a sippy cup, and eating Cheerios because he is over six feet tall.

All the Things

It is quite frankly a "Lose Lose" situation for us control freaks.

There is no way around it.

So, there I was, sitting on my hands, and using all my acting skills and deep breathing techniques, and imagining I was a professional driving instructor.

It is so much easier to think I am someone getting paid to die versus someone who is just choosing to tempt death on a regular basis.

But then it slowly happened. The deep breathing started to work.

There was a calm car with no distractions.

The new driver was listening and cautious.

The images of death stopped flashing in my head.

I realized this was one of those milestones I had heard about. One of those experiences when you are in the years of toddling and potty training that seems so very far away.

All the Things

It is like thinking of walking on another alien planet when you are barely breathing on the Mars terrain you are newly experiencing. It was one those stories I had only heard about from other more seasoned parents. One that when our babies were barely crawling was painful to think about. Yet here I was, sitting shotgun to a young man with full-on facial hair who seemed to only yesterday be happy with his Thomas sippy cup in the back.

Sitting shotgun used to be so exciting. Not so much now.

The control is *gone*.

I don't know about you, but we didn't have the funds to upgrade our Sienna with the tandem pedal and brake systems. So, we just risk it. Every single time.

And there I was, sitting shotgun and giving ever so calming directions.

"So, here is a sign that is telling you that a stop light is coming up.

Take your foot off the accelerator now.

All the Things

Start braking now.

Good job.

Okay, so put your blinker on now, and check your mirrors now.

Here comes a blinking four way stop. What is the rule for this? Who goes first?"

You get the idea.

Our new driver was focused on the road ahead. He had checked his mirrors, was wearing his seatbelt, didn't have the music on, and we were heading out of town on a two-way highway.

Up until this time he had been driving around town. The speed limits were more controlled. There were areas where he could pull off if need be. There were parking lots where he could pull off and rest if he needed. There were destinations I could pretend we were heading to so I could take over and tell him good job.

But once we headed out of town, there was something he hadn't encountered yet. I hadn't thought of it either. I had not really remembered it because I had been driving for so long, but once I saw it, I made sure to tell him.

"So, buddy, you know how sometimes you hug that white line on the right?"

"Yeah," he said while staring straight ahead.

"Okay, well up until now, you have had a shoulder to kind of have some wiggle room if you go a little too far. But now you don't have that.

Do you see that gravel on the side?"

"Yeah," he answered.

"Well, that is called a soft shoulder. If you go over the line here, it is very risky because it is easier to lose control of the car when the wheels hit that going quickly. "

"Okay," he countered.

I could see his focus get more intense.

All the Things

I continued to breathe deeply and wondered if my life insurance was paid up in full.

His hands were firmly gripping the steering wheel when he had something to say.

"Hey Mom?"

"Yeah, buddy. What is it? You're doing a great job."

"I don't think I want to drive home," he said quietly.

"Okay? Why is that?" I asked.

"I don't like driving without the guard rails."

Folks, here is the thing. Every day, parenting is driving *without* the guard rails. Sure, we have support systems, we have friends who we can call, but really, we all are just driving along hoping we don't hit that soft shoulder and start barreling out of control.

And many times, in life, *we will*.

Our lives will come to a stop for reasons out of our control. Just like a flat tire on a car, things in our lives will go flat—relationships, jobs, dreams that were once so important.

All the Things

There will be times when we hit that soft shoulder and things will *spin out of control*. We will crash. Hopefully nothing will burn. Things will become broken and unrepairable. We will get bruises and need physical therapy, or emotional support.

It is hard to keep driving in the middle of those lines. However, we also have to remember we have support that comes in a different form.

My boy was seeing that life is easier with the guard rails. It is easier when we have a strong shoulder to keep us on course. We have both in a daily relationship with the one who guards our comings and goings. Psalm 128:1 says, "The LORD will watch over your coming and going both now and forevermore." He is your guard rail and he is stronger than any metal barrier we can imagine.

And when you have found yourself spun out? What then? He has the strongest shoulder for us to rely on when our route gets weary. In Isaiah 40:28-31 it says, "Have you not known? Have you not heard? The God Who lives forever is the Lord, the

One Who made the ends of the earth. He will not become weak or tired. His understanding is too great for us to begin to know. He gives strength to the weak. And He gives power to him who has little strength. Even very young men get tired and become weak and strong young men trip and fall. But they who wait upon the Lord will get new strength. They will rise up with wings like eagles. They will run and not get tired. They will walk and not become weak."

So, my friend, just like my son was realizing that driving without the rails is scary, we may find ourselves in a place where we feel like we are driving alone. However, we are never alone. God will always be there helping us to keep our eyes on the road in front of us. He will help to give us signs to guide the way. His light will shine when the sun goes down and darkness comes. We must just rely on Him and he will show us the way.

He is the ultimate GPS for those who follow him. We don't even need cell service to have him reach us. Even when we may turn him off and think we know the way; he is always there when we decide to let him lead our lives again. He recalculates, over and over, and over again. He is ever patient with us as we navigate the roads we are on. Because he is faithful, he keeps showing us signs for exits we should take or routes we should avoid. He knows the roads that will lead us safely home.

God **P**romises **S**alvation.

17
THE ART OF LISTENING

One thing we know for sure on this journey of parenting is kids pay attention. They really do, even though we would not always bet our last piece of Dove dark chocolate on it. I honestly never even put much thought into how many times I would repeat myself as a parent. It really wasn't on my new mom radar *at all*. It wasn't one of the things I prepared for. Luckily, it is one of those skills that gets honed over time. Repeating.

At first you just do it a few times here and there. And when children are younger, we do it because we know they are learning and are picking up so much new information. They obviously need to hear something more than once to build those listening and comprehension muscles. We do this so many times a day, it is no wonder by the time they are tweens and teens that we desire quiet. At least I do.

At the end of the day, my brain is so tired from talking. I feel I have said ALL THE THINGS, yet not really gotten anything of substance out. It is like reciting the alphabet 489 times, but not really putting meaningful words together. At such times in my day, I feel a desert island or a soaking tub in a sound proof bathroom would be bliss. However, since I have no such time for island jaunts, and wedging myself into our small 1960's tub would lead to major chiropractic visits, a solo trip to the local Aldi has to suffice as therapy.

From the time they are little, kids hear things we don't think they will. They seem inconsequential in the day-to-day comings and goings of our household life. They hear that bag of chips being ever so quietly opened after they've been tucked in. Can't we snack in peace? Suddenly that sound propels them into the spirals of hunger and unquenchable thirst. They need to go to the bathroom. Cue the litany of nighttime stalling techniques.

Similarly, their ears are verbal sponges. They soak up the word or phrase you said, *just one time* when you accidentally stubbed your toe on the corner of your metal bed frame. Sweet Jesus that hurt! You thought you were safe from their youthful ears, but no.

They heard that phrase clearly even when they were in their room playing with Legos. Now they can repeat it with the same inflection and passion that a method actor does in an Oscar nominated film. It has proven quite embarrassing when Walmart becomes their stage and the cashier's eyes of judgment are as piercing as any movie critic's negative review.

Kids have a knack for remembering the things we *don't* want them to. However, it is equally amazing to me that when I speak directly to them with no other distractions or persons in our company, it is as if my words take on a completely different language from my native tongue. These precious children I love deeply, look at me with eyes of confusion as if Swahili or Javanese

has emanated from my usual English-speaking mouth.

Or perhaps like mine, your children look past you when

you're trying with all the clarity and patience you can muster, to

explain what chores need to be done prior to earning their "tech

time." Their eyes take on an eerie blank stare, as if their bodies

have been hijacked by a mind-controlling villain from the future.

We tell them it is important to listen. It is important to use

their "listening ears." It is important to pay attention. Stay

focused. What they hear is, "Blah, blah, blah." If our lives were

instantly turned into a cartoon, our voice would sound

surprisingly like Charlie Brown's teacher. Poor woman. All she

wanted was to help teach her students. She could have been

reciting the ABC's for all that Charlie heard.

As children get older, what we hope they are listening to

becomes more important. It is no longer, "Don't put that in your

mouth" or explaining how to tie their shoes. It bypasses even how

to change a tire, or the importance of sharing with their siblings. It is no longer about how throwing toys is not nice, but why texting and driving is very unsafe and dangerous. The need for them to truly be listening becomes much more life altering if they don't and life giving if they do.

Recently, we were on a family trip back to upstate New York and visiting extended family. We were touring many local museums and attractions while also spending a lot of time with cousins and family as well. While meeting one of my oldest and dearest friends for dinner, she offered to be our tour guide for a trip to New York City. We jumped at the chance for her expertise as she and her family visit the city regularly and know the ways to navigate it with greater ease.

We spent time mapping out what attractions we wanted to see and talked to the children about what an exciting time we were going to have. We were all so pumped about spending the day seeing and doing ALL THE THINGS the city had to offer.

Our day started out perfectly with our two-hour drive to the city going smoothly. We started our trek to the Museum of

All the Things

Natural History and took our first of many subway trains that day. The museum was absolutely amazing, and we all were in awe of the beautiful artistic representations of all the exhibits. We had explained to the children about the need for all of us to stick together. We had six people so we all should always have a buddy. All was going well. (For those of you who are reading and simultaneously analyzing my literary style, note the use of the past tense was.)

After our next stop, we were casually waiting for our next train when my friend used the time to mention something to our family. She said, "I just want to talk to you about something that happened to our family. I am sure we won't have to deal with it and it only happened once to us, but it just popped in my head and I wanted to make sure to mention it."

She continued, "Sometimes certain stops are more crowded than others. At certain times of the day, some stops are more crowded than others. So, if we somehow get separated, maybe because we can't all get on the train at that stop, or we get pushed out of the train before our stop because there are too many people, don't panic."

At this point I decided that internally it was time to panic!

I would like it duly noted this was *not* one of the things I had considered for this trip. I am not a daily subway user, so I hadn't even thought of this possible scenario.

I was listening intently as she continued, "If we get separated, and you get left at the platform, just get on the next train and get off at the next stop. We will get off at the next stop and wait for you. However, if you panic and don't know what to do next, just stay put. One of us will come back for you."

Honestly, I was not really prepared for this little nugget of helpful city navigation. My naive noncity momma mind had never considered this. But she nonchalantly added, "I am sure we will all be able to stick together just fine, but I just felt I needed to share this."

At that point our train arrived, and we all got on with no issues. I took a big deep breath and decided to not let that nugget of information cause undue stress and steal my joy and excitement

of exploring the city. This is something I must intentionally work

at because I am by nature a worrier. However, after all, she said

not to worry, and she came here all the time. So, we continued

with our city adventure.

About an hour later we all were heading from Central

Park to Battery Park to see the Statue of Liberty. We loaded on the

train and were somewhat spread out on the last car of our train. I

was standing with my younger son talking, while my friend sat

with my daughter in a seat. My husband and my oldest son were

standing together by the door of the train.

We had about four stops to go before departing the train,

so we were enjoying the experience. Little did I notice that after

the first stop, my oldest son was now on the other side of my

friend as more people had boarded and he moved down for them

to have space. My husband was crowded near the door as more

people had boarded.

All the Things

At the next stop, when the door opened, my husband decided to step out so the crowd of riders who needed to get off had more space. At that same time, my oldest son saw his dad step off and thought our stop had arrived, so he exited the train at the other door. He started walking toward my husband who by then had re-boarded the train.

At this point, I was chatting casually with a mom and her daughter while still standing with my other son and was utterly unaware of the situation. It wasn't until I heard pounding on the glass door and recognized it as my husband's voice yelling that I became aware of the situation. He was screaming and pounding, "GET ON THE NEXT TRAIN, AND GET OFF AT THE NEXT STOP!"

And that was when I saw him.

Our oldest son was on the other side of the glass subway door. He was standing looking through the glass, unable to get in, and then the train slowly headed to its next stop.

All the Things

At this point, my brain was finally putting all the pieces together and realizing my fifteen-year-old son was on his own, in the middle of New York City.

To truly grasp the depth of my fear, you must also know this small nugget of helpful technological insight.

My son was phone free.

Yup, you read that right. I had taken my teenage son to one of the *largest* metropolitan cities in the *entire world* without his cell phone. We had taken away the phone earlier in the spring due to issues with usage and didn't want to reintroduce it while visiting family back east for fear it would be a distraction from connecting with family. What I thought would be a good decision turned out to be something I then, in that instant, began second guessing.

Immediately, the mom who had been standing next to my other son and myself started talking to me. She started her litany of questions, "OH my God! What are you going to do? What kind of a kid is he? Is he freaking out right now? Are you freaking out right now? Do you think he is panicking right now? Will he know

what to do?" I remained outwardly silent although the voices in

my head were deafening.

She continued her barrage of questions to my younger son.

"What kind of brother is he? Is he a kid who has anxiety or is he

calm? How do you think he is handling this?"

My son, with complete deadpan said, "Well he hasn't

hugged me in like five years, so he is pretty chill."

The lady laughed uncomfortably and asked me, "What are

you going to do?"

Honestly what could I do?

This situation was out of my hands.

I was not in control.

I did know however, that my response could affect my

other son and his anxiety of such an experience. But he was right,

humor was a better course of action than panic.

All the Things

I looked at her calmly and said, "It will all work out." I smiled a gentle momma smile and could hardly believe the words uttered from my lips.

She too looked shocked, as her stare continued blankly. I believe she thought I was a crazy woman who had just left her son to start an early career of street pedaling. I think she was also silently having my face burn in her memory so she could report me to the NYPD.

Before I knew it, the train had stopped again, and my party of five of the six departed. We all stood together and formulated our plan. We decided to spread out on the platform with my two other children with myself and my friend, while my husband went further up the platform to better have a chance to see my son *if* he did indeed get on the next train and find us here.

You see, it all comes down to listening. Had he been listening to my friend? Had he been paying attention? Did he see his dad screaming at him through the glass and really *hear* his words? Or had the words sounded like Charlie Brown's teacher?

All the Things

Had he been focusing on something he thought was more important? Had there been something rolling around in my son's mind that caused him to not hear the message our friend had been trying to pass on?

Before my mind could go down the rabbit hole of worry, the next train pulled up. The doors opened and off stepped my oldest son. He casually walked toward us, and my momma lungs finally started breathing again. However, I played it cool and collected. I said, "Hey, you good?"

"Yup, I'm good," he said in his chill teenager voice. He was exactly like his little brother had predicted he would be.

As the rest of the day continued, we chatted about the experience and how he felt when he was by himself. He said he was a little like, "Gosh, I can't believe they actually left me." But he remembered what my friend had told him to do, and he did it. In the end, it all worked out to be an adventure with a lesson learned. It is something none of us will ever forget, and we had a great uneventful rest of our day in the city.

All the Things

After heading home and having time to reflect on our experience on the subway, it made me start to think about our journey in life and how similar it is to the day we had in the city. You see, people in our lives often impart anecdotes or stories to us and we can choose what to do with this information. We can take to heart those stories and use them to our advantage, or we can ignore them and try to find our own way blindly navigating the subways of life.

As parents, we hope the lessons and words we give our children are soaked up and used wisely when the need arises. We know there will be a time when we are not able to be with our children. We hope they can regain composure and not panic. That they will think clearly and rationally when these times arise. They will have experiences where we are not physically with them. We pray they will remember our guidance and make the right choices. On this day, my son did just that. It was a happy ending.

However, some of our children will be separated from us because they purposely choose to step off the train. They feel they know best and want to venture away from the way our family

chooses to parent or live life. This is a very painful part of

parenting because just like I was not in control of how the events

of the day were unfolding, neither are parents of children

rebelling against familial rules.

The only choice we have as parents during these times is to

rely on God's grace to cover our children and continue to love

them fiercely. For all of us at one time or another have not

listened to the words that have been lovingly given to us. Even

though God's word tells all of us what we need to do in times of

suffering or trial we are deaf to his words. If we just listened, like

we wish our children would do, oh how much more disciplined

children we would be too. If we weren't distracted by what the

world is telling us is important, we wouldn't be missing the train

either.

Matthew 6:25 says, "Therefore I tell you, do not worry

about your life, what you will eat or drink; or about your body, what you will wear." However, I struggle with worrying about

these *exact* types of things day after day. Why am I not listening?

However, God continues to be patient with me. He keeps

repeating his word repeatedly through the encounters we have

with people placed in our lives. He is ever so patient with us long

after our mere mortal brains would have given up. His parenting

of us is perfect. He sends us the next train--Always. We must be

the one who chooses to step on.

God also tells us in Joshua 1:9, "This is my command—be

strong and courageous! Do not be afraid or discouraged. For the

Lord your God is with you wherever you go." I felt this verse

speak clearly with me on that subway car. There was a peace I felt

that was so different than I had experienced before.

I should have been freaking out! I should have been

panicking. This is what mothers do when their children are

separated from them in a city of 8.623 million people. But I wasn't

freaking out. I was rooting myself deep in my faith that this event

was a lesson my son needed to experience. I had no control of the situation, so I rested, albeit not easily, in knowing God was with him. He was not alone. He was not unseen. He was covered.

Some of the lessons our children need to learn cannot happen when we are with them. In fact, we won't be there for most of the lessons they need to experience. As young moms this is foreign territory to us, because we are so used to being right there. We are next to the toddler who is navigating their first steps or new foods. We are right behind the three-year-old who is making the first of many trips up the slide at the playground. In the beginning, that toddler seems so small and that slide seems ten feet tall.

They will have to navigate many trains on their own. We are preparing for these challenges. We want them to go bravely forth in this glorious world we are all sharing. We want them to spread their wings, take flight, and be courageous. They need not panic, but know they are covered with the best guidance and grace their perfect Heavenly Father has for them.

All the Things

Think about the stories people have shared with you recently, were you too distracted to listen to them? Would they have kept you from experiencing difficult situations if you would have just listened? What words have you listened intently to and how did they change the course of your train ride?

We need to actively tell those stories to others. When you feel that little voice telling you to share a story, do it. On that memorable day in the city, my friend surely did. She had no idea her words would be so needed shortly after they left her mouth. However, her words not only gave my son his direction, they also helped me know she had walked before me. She gave me the peace of knowing that I could navigate this scary time. It was going to be okay.

Her words filled the ears of my dear son and brought him back to us. He was given the direction by others. These directions had never occurred to his father or me because we had never navigated these parental waters before. Our son had to take the necessary steps all on his own. God also has given us all the wisdom and guidance we need. We all need to listen more and make the choices we know are best. When we do, the ride on the train will take us to wonderful places.

18
A MAJESTIC LIFE

Horses. Tigers. Dolphins. What do these animals have in common? No, it is not that they all are mammals. It is not that they all are found in the wild. When I see these animals, there is one word that comes to mind.

Majestic.

According to Google, for something to be majestic it must have or show great beauty or dignity.

When these animals are in their element, they are beautiful creatures that are one with their environment. They are doing what they were created to do. There is true beauty there and one that cannot be replicated by man.

All the Things

The horse, when on the open plains, does not have to think hard about galloping. They are not manipulating their muscles to do what needs to be done. Their hooves beat the ground in perfect rhythm and create an equine orchestra that has sounded in our country since the 1500's. Their speed and skill are not forced. It is what they do. They excel at it.

Likewise, the tiger does not need to put new stripes on to blend in. He or she does not have the urge to be who they are not. They are stealthy and smooth with the Creator's camouflage. Their ability to move in silence is not because of sulkiness or selfishness. It is who they are hard-wired to be; they do not lose sleep over wishing they were a lion.

In addition, the bottle-nosed dolphin, while exploring the Atlantic coast, does not worry if their aerial is a perfect arch compared to their pod mates. They do not wonder if their whistles and clicks are too loud or annoying. They do what they were created to do. They show joy and exhilaration in the riding of waves because they simply can; they do it well.

All the Things

When we look at these creatures it seems like they hold some magical power. They race and pounce; they glide and frolic. However, they are simply doing what they were created to do. There is no magic. There is no filter we are seeing them through that changes what we see. We are seeing the true essence of living a life for the purpose it is intended.

However, many of us lose sight of what our gifts and talents are. Or maybe we were never told we even have them. Our gifts are still waiting to be opened. Our Creator has patiently been waiting for us to peel back the wrapping to uncover the perfect present he has in us.

Instead of finding those gifts and putting them on, and wearing them confidently like a favorite comfortable sweatshirt, we become entrenched in a battle between what the world tells us we should do or become.

We become conflicted by what the world wants to hear and what our heart longs to sing. We listen to the whispering of others rather than hear the true music of our Creator. We just live-day by day-minute by minute.

However, when we start on the journey to peel away the unnecessary distractions in our lives, we find the essence of who we were created to be. There is no need for muscles and stripes that are not ours because ours are truly enough. They have always been enough.

We all have been blessed by certain gifts God has bestowed upon us. When we can sit down in the quiet and unwrap our boxes then we can truly see. We can marvel at the gifts. We can look clearly at who we were created to be, and we can start using our talents and gifts to glorify God. We can boldly begin to serve others who need to be encouraged.

In Romans 12:4-8 Living Bible (TLB) it says:

"Just as there are many parts to our bodies, so it is with Christ's body. We are all parts of it, and it takes every one of us to make it complete, for we each have different work to do. So, we belong to each other, and each needs all the others. God has given each of us the ability to do certain things well. So, if God has given you the ability to prophesy, then prophesy whenever you can—as often as your faith is strong enough to receive a message from God.

If your gift is that of <u>serving others,</u> serve them well. If you are a <u>teacher,</u> do a good job of teaching. If you are a <u>preacher,</u> see to it that your sermons are strong and helpful. If God has given you money,<u> be generous in helping others with it</u>. If God has given you<u> administrative ability</u> and put you in charge of the work of others, take the responsibility seriously. Those who<u> offer comfort to the sorrowing</u> should do so with Christian cheer."

So how were you knit together? What breaks your heart

and makes it beat all at the same time? Are you someone with the

gift of prophecy, who can see a situation and clearly see the path

God is wanting to be taken? Who needs to have you in their

court? How can you help others to navigate things in a Godly

way?

Perhaps you have a servant's heart. Do you find joy in

helping others and seeing how their needs can be met? Are you

the type of person who always signs up to bring food to the new

mom or family with an illness? What organizations would benefit

from your heart for service?

Do learning and teaching make your heart sing? Do you

have examples to share with others that will help them see things more clearly? Do you like to walk alongside someone and help them navigate the paths of life and learning? Then you have been given the gift of teaching. How can you share this with others?

How has faith worked in your life? What has your journey been like? How has God worked to manifest his plan for you? Can you see how others would benefit from feeling that in their lives? Perhaps your experiences are just the foundation of a pastoral calling. A calling to share how God has transformed your heart and molded it to now help others with restorative work.

Are you a business person who has been gifted with amazing ideas that allow your bank account to be full and then some? How are you using your blessings to help others and show them that God is walking right beside them?

If you are a person in an administrative job, how are you leading your people? Are you doing so in such a way that you are modeling God's love for all your workers? Do you think of them all as sacred creations of his majestic artistry? How are you showing them their worth? How can you do it better?

All the Things

Do you have a heart for the broken-hearted or those who suffer and see no hope? Then serve them with all the fabric of your heart. Fear not what others think and sit with them in the trenches. You have the gifts to root yourself down and give comfort to others. You are a blessing to those you walk beside.

Many of us never realized that instead of looking at what we should be when we grow up, we should rather be seeking what seeds were already planted long before we even opened our eyes as adults. Instead of comparing ourselves to the most popular trending job descriptions, we need to look at our hearts and how they beat. We need to choose things that go in step with how we were divinely created in the first place.

However, many of us just didn't realize it. Maybe we were too busy wishing we were a lion.

When we find our true purpose and start living it each day without fail, when we match what we were created to be with what we are doing, our life and the lives of others will be changed. That truly is a majestic life.

All the Things

REFERENCES

Goldberg, Joel. "It takes A Village To Determine The Origins of An African Proverb." NPR. July 30, 2016. www.npr.org.

Mecking, Olga. "The Incredible Post-Birth Service All Dutch Women Receive." 2016. www.babble.com.

Olsen, Melissa. "International Postpartum Traditions." March 20, 2017. Utah Doula Association. www.utahdoulas.org

DIGGING DEEPER:
Questions for Small Groups/Book Clubs

1. Have you ever felt you were judging other moms in their parenting journey? What was your "payoff" for judging them? How can you be more understanding when you find yourself in similar situations in the future? Have you felt the eyes of judgment on you because of parenting choices you have made? How have you reacted to these outside perspectives? Are you proud of how you handled these encounters? By taking away the emotional component, what could you learn from these perspectives that could benefit your current parenting methodology? Read Luke 6:37-42, James 4:11-12, and Philippians 2:3. How do these verses speak to how we should treat one another on our parenting journeys?

2. In Chapter 2, "The Creation of A Non-Judgmental Parent," Schindler speaks candidly about sleep deprivation and reacting with anger. It is easy to understand how both can play out in households of all types. Have you ever found yourself so tired you can't believe what has come out of your mouth? How do you reel yourself back in when you find yourself in these types of situations? Do you apologize to your spouse and/or children after these types of encounters? What can you do to make sure you recover from these types of situations with grace for all involved? Read Ephesians 4:32 and James 1:19. How can we strive to live these out in real time?

3. In Chapter 3, "Supermoms," Schindler writes about the many talents that moms possess. However, often we look at our shortcomings or how we aren't measuring up instead of focusing on what we are doing well. In what areas of your life do you feel gifted? What areas of life, even the small ones, do

you feel positive about? Do you mention to other moms what areas of their lives you see them succeeding in? If not, how can you be more observant and help lift other moms up? Read 1 Thessalonians 5:11 and Ephesians 4:29. How do these verses support a culture of lifting others up?

4. In Chapter 4, "Sticky Situations" Schindler writes, "...we *all* find ourselves in these situations. We have great ideas of certain paths, or jobs, or relationships working out. We eagerly see how it all will work out for our benefit and bless our lives and the lives of those around us. We don't always think through the exact routes of exit if things go south." When have you encountered situations like these? How did you come to the realization these choices weren't the right path for you? How do you handle seeing other people you love making choices you know aren't God's best plans for them? How do you love them unconditionally and what does this look like? How does God show you are loved even when you are acting very childlike in your actions?

5. In Chapter 5, "Visions of Perfection," Schindler shares the story of being drawn to the photograph of a little girl. She talks about listening to the whisperings that at first didn't make sense to her and how it all came together years after her daughter was born. John 15:4 says, "Abide in Me, and I in you. As the branch is not able to bear fruit of itself unless it abides in the vine, so neither you, unless you abide in Me." Have there been times in your life you have felt tugs to follow a path or complete a journey for a reason that wasn't clear in the present time? When have you been asked to continue, to abide, and you decided to just stop? How have those times in your life affected your role as a parent, spouse, or friend? What do you feel the words "Abide in Me" mean on a day-to-day basis? How can you live this out in your interactions with others?

6. Chapter 6 is entitled "Puppy Love" and it delves deeply into the balancing act of protecting the hearts of our children and ourselves from loss and what we truly will lose by not experiencing the love and world God has given us. Schindler writes, "It can't work both ways. We can't both live in darkness and shine light at the same time." Do you struggle with becoming overwhelmed with the sadness and darkness of this world? How do you right yourself and focus on being the light rather than being engulfed in the darkness? How do you shine the light in the lives of others? What do John 16:33 and Joshua 1:9 tell us to do in times of trial and tribulation?

7. In Chapter 7, "Building with Direction," Schindler writes, "We are always on the lookout for the next best thing. We tell ourselves this will make us happy. This will give us contentment. This will make things better and more exciting. The world tells us this is all so." Do you struggle with getting caught up in "the next big thing" in your life? Can you specifically identify things you continue reaching for? How does this constant need for attainment affect your life and relationships? Read 1 Timothy 6:6-12. How does this give a blueprint for how we are to handle this daily pursuit?

8. Chapter 8, "Batter Up" states, "But some of our children battle oppressors we weren't prepared to face." What areas of your parenting journey do you feel you were gravely unprepared for? How has this affected your emotional health? How has this affected your relationships with others? What support has helped you be effective at parenting a child with unique needs? Do you and your spouse share the same concerns or perspective with the needs of this child? How does this affect your relationship?

9. In Chapter 10, "A Woman I Know," Schindler starts writing as if she is mentioning different people who interact with her children. However, the reader is soon clued in that she is referring to the various facets of her personality that exist within parenting. There is a balance of both positive and negative types of interactions with her children. She writes, "Her voice becomes harsh and quick and her eyes pulse with irritation. She slays those same children with words of anger that slice and wound their tender hearts. Those words would never make it on her social media feed, and those eyes wouldn't be uploaded as her new profile pic." Can you relate to this honesty? Do you find yourself dealing with similar situations as a parent? Do you speak openly and honestly to other moms about these types of situations? Do you feel you can be honest with other moms in your current circle? How do you balance the emotions that come and go with such interactions? What healthy things do you do to keep your mind, body, and words in harmony with how you want to parent?

10. Chapter 11, "Your Voice," delves deeply in to feeling "lost" in motherhood. Schindler writes, "There comes times when as a mother we feel lost. We feel we are talking but nothing of any significant value is coming out. It is not that our loved ones are not listening. It is just our "voice" has lost its depth. It has forgotten the tune that used to make our heart skip. If you have felt this way, or are feeling this way now, fear not. You can find your voice again. You can find what makes your soul sing." What gifts and talents do you have that have laid dormant for a while? What dreams did you once have? Are they attainable in any form in the season of motherhood you are currently living? How can you carve out time for yourself and nurture things which once made your heart feel full? Make a list of those things that once made you happy.

11. Chapter 12, entitled "Our Villages" talks about the need for

community in our parenting journey and the various post-partum customs from around the world. Do you have any unique circumstances of how you experienced postpartum? Was this a relaxing time or filled with other positive experiences? Did you suffer from postpartum depression or other pregnancy/delivery complications that made post birth a traumatic or difficult time? Who are the villagers in your life? How do these people pour into you? If you haven't found your community as a mother, what local groups could you tap into so you aren't navigating these waters alone? How are you a villager in other people's lives? Read Proverbs 3:5 and John 15:13. How can these verses help you to support others and be supported?

12. "Our Villages" also speaks about our American culture and the expectation that moms should give birth and head out to their local "Target" to get back into the role of life. How do you feel this expectation affects the emotional and physical wellbeing of new and seasoned moms? What other social or media "norms" play into our views of what motherhood looks like? How does the media manipulate the image of motherhood and what it should be, "if we are doing it right?" How can we counter this on a day-to-day basis? How has this viewpoint affected your personal journey as a mom? Have you fallen victim to just "sucking it up?" What internal struggles has this ignited?

13. An area of parenting that many moms do not anticipate is the "triggering" of past experiences which may be brought on by experiences our children are now having that remind us of past hurts or trauma. Have you had these past issues affect your parenting journey? If so, how did you navigate these feelings? Did it affect your ability to parent effectively? Has it affected the relationship with your children? How has recognizing being "triggered" by these events helped you in positive ways in your parenting?

14. In Chapter 13, "A Balanced Climb," Schindler states, "Unfortunately, the reality is the more we add to our balancing act, the more certain plates fall. They break and are not replaced. This is fine for hobbies like scrapbooking and knitting. Those plates don't have hearts." As a mother, do you feel you have too many plates spinning? How does that balancing act affect your day to day life? How does it affect your relationships with your children? What is the rationale for having so many plates spinning? Is it adding value to your life or taking away from it? How can you narrow down what needs to be done versus all that you are committing to? How would your life look if you made these changes? How does this make you feel?

15. In Chapter 13, "A Balanced Climb," Schindler also writes about the need for moms to get away. She shares, "But the crux of the issue is, when we *don't* take the time, the balance is so off kilter we aren't able to do anything well. Everything we do is off and can look a lot like a rider on a bike with a wobbly wheel, or sound like a ballad without a chorus. We are plugging away, but we are *not* pulled together. We don't think clearly or parent with patience..." How do you make time for yourself? What gives you the fuel you need to nourish your soul? How do you balance this with all the responsibilities and demands in your life? What advice can you give about how you make this time happen consistently? If it isn't happening, how could you make it happen?

16. Chapter 13 continues by saying, "It is the same when we clean out our hearts from the excess and superfluous. Taking stock of what we are carrying and why allows us to clear things out. Our journey from there on does tend to feel lighter. It makes moving forward and going to new places a lot easier. We can move forward without the heaviness of being held back by that which was never there to be helpful on our

journey in the first place." For many of us, we also are carrying past hurts and grief of things unspoken. These are ten-ton invisible weights that will eventually bring us down. What things are you carrying in your heart that you need to clean out? What things are weighing you down from truly experiencing the relationships in your life and all that God wants for you?

17. Chapter 14, "$151.20" shares an extraordinary example of God showing up and being ever faithful in Schindler's ability to get her wedding rings sized when the financial means to do so wasn't in the budget. Do you have examples of how God has worked in your life in either small "jewelry sizing" ways or big momentous ways? If these events have happened to you, do you share them with others? Have you traveled through seasons of your life when you lost your faith or were just plain searching for God's presence in it at all? Read Lamentations 3:22-23, 2 Timothy 2:13, and Deuteronomy 31:6. Discuss how we can rely on God's faithfulness daily. How will this affect your parenting and other relationships?

18. In Chapter 15, "Gratitude Pie," Schindler writes, "Our ability to connect so quickly through technology often takes away the actual art of *real* connectivity." Do you feel you have authentic connections with friends and loved ones? How do you make this happen? If you don't, how could you? Do you feel technology helps or hampers this? How do you make intentional time to spend with your children and spouse? Do you have certain traditions, habits, or boundaries that help you to do this?

19. Chapter 16 entitled "Guard Rails" chronicles Schindler's perspective as a parent of a new driver. What stories can you

share about parenting during this time? What advice can you give about supporting new drivers in healthy ways while still giving them independence? Do you have any funny stories of new driving situations you can share?

20. "Guard Rails" continues on a more serious note with, "Our lives will come to a stop for reasons out of our control. Just like a flat tire on a car, things in our lives will go flat--- relationships, jobs, and dreams that were once so important. There will be times when we hit that soft shoulder and things will *spin out of control.*" Have you experienced times in your life when things have spun out of control? How did you navigate the emotions and reality with this experience? Looking back now did you handle the situation in a way that brings you peace? If not, are there things you can do today that could bring closure and healing to this situation? Have you had to help other friends navigate these difficult types of life experiences? How do you support your friends in real ways or how did other people support you during these trying times? How could they have supported you differently?

21. In Chapter 17, "The Art of Listening," Schindler pulls no punches in reminding us that we are much like our own children. She writes, "For all of us at one time or another have not listened to the words that have been lovingly given to us. Even though God's word tells all of us what we need to do in times of suffering or trial we are deaf to his words." What do you do in your day-to-day life to truly be attentive to God's voice? How would making that time and devotion to him alleviate your fears and worries? How will this focus help you as a mother, spouse, and friend? Read Psalm 116:1-2. How can you make this verse part of your family devotion and focus? How will it help your children to rely on Him when you are not "on the train" with them?

22. Chapter 17 also mentions, "Think about the stories people
    have shared with you recently that you were too distracted to
    listen to. Would they have kept you from experiencing
    difficult situations if you would have just listened? What
    words have you listened intently to and how did they change
    the course of your train ride? We need to actively tell those
    stories to others." When have you had someone share a
    situation with you that helped you navigate an event you
    didn't see coming? How would your life have been different,
    or your reaction changed had you not had the benefit of their
    wisdom?

23. What is the difference in being a friend to another mom and
    sharing wisdom versus just telling them your opinion? How
    do you react when others try to be helpful in giving advice?
    How do you receive that gesture? How could you better
    position your heart to receive it in the future? Is there a
    specific person who you need to extend grace to when they
    approach you with their version of "wisdom?" Is there
    someone who you know needs you to approach them
    differently?

24. Chapter 18, "A Majestic Life" says, "Many of us never
    realized that instead of looking at what we should be when
    we grow up, we should rather be seeking what seeds were
    already planted long before we even opened our eyes as
    adults. Instead of comparing ourselves to the most popular
    trending job descriptions, we need to look at our hearts and
    how they beat. Then we need to choose things that go in step

with how we were divinely created in the first place." As we continue to help guide our children into the roles of young adulthood and being independent, how do you encourage them to really look at what their gifts and talents are? How do you support them in navigating what will truly recognize their gifts and talents? What resources have you used to navigate those waters? What advice could you give new moms when those far-off years seem so distant and quite frankly painful to think about?

25. Chapter 18, ends with, "When we find our true purpose and start living it each day without fail, we too will be witness to majesty right here in our own lives. When we match what we were created to be with what we are doing, our life and the lives of others will be changed. That truly is a majestic life." Do you feel you are living in alignment with your true God-given gifts? If so, how do you use those daily?

~NOTES~

All the Things

ENCOURAGEMENT FOR YOUR DAILY WALK

I hope you have found *All the Things* both a comfort and an encouragement. I want you to know that you are not alone on this journey of motherhood. As you read, you encountered various scriptural references. Although there is nothing that can replace really digging in and reading God's word, I wanted to give you a quick reference section for the scripture that was mentioned. These are a just a few verses that I have found comforting in times of both frustration and fear and nourishing in times of "parental dehydration."

These verses are listed in order of how they were mentioned throughout the book so they can also serve as a quick reference for those using the "Digging Deeper: Book Study Questions." I have taken these from a couple different translations including the New Living Translation (NLV), the New International Version (NIV), and The Living Bible (TLB).

In addition, the NIV Quest Study Bible is the translation which I have found to be a very helpful style of the Bible. It offers both historical and geographical information with maps, and cultural references which allow the reader to fully understand the context of time and place. There have been many times I have questioned something I have read in terms of wondering where and why things were mentioned. In the study bible format, along the margins, there is often the same question with an explanation of both context and historical accuracy.

- **Ephesians 6:10-17(NIV)**

  "[10] Finally, be strong in the Lord and in his mighty power. [11] Put on the full armor of God, so that you can take your stand against the devil's schemes. [12] For our struggle is not against flesh and blood, but against the rulers, against the authorities, against the powers of this dark world and against the spiritual forces of evil in the heavenly realms. [13] Therefore put on the full armor of God, so that when the day of evil comes, you may be able to stand your ground, and after you have done everything, to stand. [14] Stand firm then, with the belt of truth buckled around your waist, with the breastplate of righteousness in place, [15] and with your feet fitted with the readiness that comes from the gospel of peace. [16] In addition to all this, take up the shield of faith, with which you can extinguish all the flaming arrows of the evil one. [17] Take the helmet of salvation and the sword of the Spirit, which is the word of God."

- **2 Corinthians 9:8 (NIV)**

  "[8] And God is able to bless you abundantly, so that in all things at all times, having all that you need, you will abound in every good work."

- **Psalm 32:8 (NLV)**

  "[8] I will instruct you and teach you in the way you should go; I will counsel you with my loving eye on you."

- **Isaiah 40:28-31 (NLV)**

  "[28] Have you not known? Have you not heard? The God Who lives forever is the Lord, the One Who made the ends of the earth. He will not become weak or tired. His understanding is too great for us to begin to know. [29] He gives strength to the weak. And He gives power to him who has little strength. [30] Even very young men get tired and become weak and strong young men trip and fall. [31] But they who wait upon the Lord will get new strength. They will rise up with wings like eagles. They will run and not get tired. They will walk and not become weak."

- **Jeremiah 29:11 (NIV)**
  "[11] For I know the plans I have for you," declares the LORD, "plans to prosper you and not to harm you, plans to give you hope and a future."

- **Psalm 120:1 (NLV)**
  "I cried to the Lord in my trouble, and He answered me."

- **Proverbs 17:17(NIV)**
  "A friend loves at all times, and a brother is born for times of adversity."

- **Proverbs 27:17(NIV)**
  "As iron sharpens iron, so one person sharpens another."

- **Proverbs 27:9 (NLT)**
  "The heartfelt counsel of a friend is as sweet as perfume and incense".

- **Matthew 6:25 (NIV)**
  "Therefore, I tell you, do not worry about your life, what you will eat or drink; or about your body, what you will wear. Is not life more than food, and the body more than clothes?"

- **Joshua 1:9 (NLT)**

  "This is my command—be strong and courageous! Do not be afraid or discouraged. For the LORD your God is with you wherever you go."

- **Romans 12:4-8 (NLV)**

  [4] Our bodies are made up of many parts. None of these parts have the same use. [5] There are many people who belong to Christ. And yet, we are one body which is Christ's. We are all different, but we depend on each other. [6] We all have different gifts that God has given to us by His loving-favor. We are to use them. If someone has the gift of preaching the Good News, he should preach. He should use the faith God has given him. [7] If someone has the gift of helping others, then he should help. If someone has the gift of teaching, he should teach. [8] If someone has the gift of speaking words of comfort and help, he should speak. If someone has the gift of sharing what he has, he should give from a willing heart. If someone has the gift of leading other people, he should lead them. If someone has the gift of showing kindness to others, he should be happy as he does it."

- **Luke 6:37-42 (NIV)**

  [37] "Do not judge, and you will not be judged. Do not condemn, and you will not be condemned. Forgive, and you will be forgiven. [38] Give, and it will be given to you. A good measure, pressed down, shaken together and running over, will be poured into your lap. For with the measure you use, it will be measured to you."
  [39] He also told them this parable: "Can the blind lead the blind? Will they not both fall into a pit? [40] The student is not above the teacher, but everyone who is fully trained will be like their teacher.
  [41] "Why do you look at the speck of sawdust in your brother's eye and pay no attention to the plank in your own eye? [42] How can you say to your brother, 'Brother, let me take the speck out of your eye,' when you

yourself fail to see the plank in your own eye? You hypocrite, first take the plank out of your eye, and then you will see clearly to remove the speck from your brother's eye."

- **James 4:11-12 (NIV)**
  [11]"Brothers and sisters, do not slander one another. Anyone who speaks against a brother or sister[a] or judges them speaks against the law and judges it. When you judge the law, you are not keeping it, but sitting in judgment on it. [12]There is only one Lawgiver and Judge, the one who is able to save and destroy. But you—who are you to judge your neighbor?"

- **Philippians 2:3 (NLV)**
  "Nothing should be done because of pride or thinking about yourself. Think of other people as more important than yourself."

- **Ephesians 4:23 (NLT)**
  "Instead, let the Spirit renew your thoughts and attitudes."

- **James 1:9 (NIV)**
  "Believers in humble circumstances ought to take pride in their high position."

- **1 Thessalonians 5:11 (NIV)**
  "Therefore encourage one another and build each other up, just as in fact you are doing."

- **Ephesians 4:29 (NIV)**
  "Do not let any unwholesome talk come out of your mouths, but only what is helpful for building others up according to their needs, that it may benefit those who listen."

- **Proverbs 3:5 (NIV)**
  "Trust in the Lord with all your heart and lean not on your own understanding."

- **John 15:13 (NIV)**
  "Greater love has no one than this: to lay down one's life for one's friends."

- **Lamentations 3:22-23 (NLT)**
  22 "The faithful love of the Lord never ends! His mercies never cease. Great is his faithfulness; his mercies begin afresh each morning."

- **2 Timothy 2:13 (NLT)**
  "If we are unfaithful, he remains faithful, for he cannot deny who he is."

- **Deuteronomy 31:6 (NLT)**
  "So be strong and courageous! Do not be afraid and do not panic before them. For the Lord your God will personally go ahead of you. He will neither fail you nor abandon you."

- **1 Timothy 6:6-12 (NIV)**
  6 But godliness with contentment is great gain. 7 For we brought nothing into the world, and we can take nothing out of it. 8 But if we have food and clothing, we will be content with that. 9 Those who want to get rich fall into temptation and a trap and into many foolish and harmful desires that plunge people into ruin and destruction. 10 For the love of money is a root of all kinds of evil. Some people, eager for money, have wandered from the faith and pierced themselves with many griefs. 11 But you, man of God, flee from all this, and pursue righteousness, godliness, faith, love, endurance and gentleness. 12 Fight the good fight of the faith. Take hold of the eternal life to which you were called when you made your good confession in the presence of many witnesses."

- **John 16:33 (NIV)**
  "I have told you these things, so that in me you may have peace. In this world you will have trouble. But take heart! I have overcome the world."

- **Josh 1:9 (NIV)**
  "Have I not commanded you? Be strong and courageous. Do not be afraid; do not be discouraged, for the LORD your God will be with you wherever you go."

- **John 15:4 (NIV)**
  "Remain in me, as I also remain in you. No branch can bear fruit by itself; it must remain in the vine. Neither can you bear fruit unless you remain in me."

- **Psalm 116:1-2 (NIV)**
  "I love the Lord, for he heard my voice; he heard my cry for mercy. Because he turned his ear to me, I will call on him as long as I live."

ABOUT THE AUTHOR

Kristen Schindler lives with her husband, Eric, and her children in southern Illinois. She was born in upstate New York where much of her extended family and favorite people still live. She loves to go back to the little river town of Coxsackie, New York where her heart feels simultaneously cupped and warmed while gazing at the Catskill Mountains.

Her youth was spent zig zagging the United States as an Air Force 'brat' together with her parents and brother, Nathan. Pieces of her heart, like breadcrumbs, have been left in various places throughout the world where she has met and found friends who have become her 'chosen family'.

She has always loved to both listen to other peoples' stories and share her own. She loves to see the connections and richness that communication and an openness to others' hearts and experiences brings to the fabric of our lives.

She is continually reminded that despite her desire to keep a firm grasp on all things she would like to control, God has positioned himself to do the driving of her life. She is merely a passenger and really, the view is much more breathtaking riding shotgun.

Made in the USA
Columbia, SC
09 February 2020

87543094R00135